Patently Silly

Daniel Wright

To Heather and Ariel –
my unique, useful and
unobvious ladies.

Patently Silly

The daftest inventions ever devised

Daniel Wright

PRION

THIS IS A PRION BOOK

Text copyright © 2008 Daniel Wright
Design copyright © 2008 Prion Books Ltd

This edition published in 2008 by Prion Books Ltd
A division of the Carlton Publishing Group
20 Mortimer Street
London W1T 3JW

A CIP catalogue for this book is available from the British Library.

ISBN 978-1-85375-684-9

For Prion Books Ltd:
Senior Editor: Gareth Jones
Editor: Cressida Malins
Art Director: Paul Chattaway
Production: Sophie Martin

For Planet Three Publishing Ltd:
Managing Editor: Lol Henderson
Editor: Andy Durrant
Designer: Paul Southcombe

Printed in China

Contents

Foreword

I am proud to call myself an inventor. When I was five years of age I couldn't write my name, but I could make the most amazing things with my Meccano set. I could identify nuts, bolts, screws, washers, spanners, gears etc., and I also had a fantastic clockwork motor. This was how I got started…

And I believe there is an invention in all of us. Sometimes what at first seems like a wacky off-the-wall idea can have a practical function in the right context, or can solve a distantly-related problem, because it approaches it from an angle that hadn't been considered before.

My advice to any prospective inventors reading this book is to give yourself the space to come up with ideas – no matter how strange they may seem at first. Then mull it over for a while. Ask yourself has it been done before? How much would it cost to make? Is there a market for it? Is there a need for it?

Most of the inventions in this book are certainly wacky, and even if they don't have a practical function, many of them could be lots of fun: the Shoe Chair on page 180, for example, would be great at a fashion show, not to mention quite amusing in the living room. As for the Aromatic Travel Mask on page 167, I could give one to my lady friend, because I smoke a pipe, and I don't want her to end up like me (I cannot tell the difference between vanilla and vindaloo). Being a dog-owner (a labrador named Ike), I'm intrigued by The Animal Garment on page 146. Not only is it the most peculiar dog vest I've ever seen, but I also wonder if it's safe for a canine to swim in. I'm also rather taken by the idea of Vehicle Shaped Caskets and Urns (page 219) too. As the owner of an E-type Jaguar I understand the passionate attachment people have for their cars. That said, I wonder if it would need road tax – the taxman is never far away, after all, and he could reason that you are going on a trip… And is it a gas or ash guzzler..?

On a more serious note, it's really, really important not to disclose a word of your idea (even to your friends) until you have protected it properly. This usually means employing a patent attorney to write up that idea, and it helps to be as well informed as you can be before you get to that stage. What do you know about intellectual property? Do you know what the word disclosure means? Do you know the difference between a patent, trademark, copyright and design registration? A trademark might be better for your idea than a patent and it doesn't cost as much. You can never do too much research, and it pays to be a little paranoid too. If you do have that good idea, make sure you sign a confidentiality agreement with whomever you end up discussing it.

But the serious business of inventing aside, I have enjoyed reading *Patently Silly*. I really believe that if you can make people laugh, then they will listen, which is why I find this book so fascinating. Also, for all the absurdity, it is, in its own wacky way, a tribute to the limitless inventiveness of the human mind.

TREVOR BAYLIS OBE

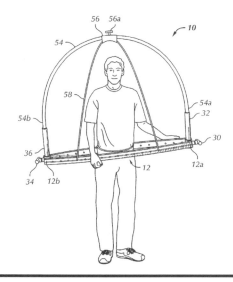

Introduction

Four years ago, in an effort to avoid financial catastrophe, I took a job assisting an inventor. My first task was to search the archives of the US Patent and Trademark Office to see if my boss's invention had already been patented. His invention was utilitarian, sane and (since I've signed a non-disclosure agreement!) not worth mentioning. It didn't prepare me for what I was about to encounter.

In the first few weeks I came across such marvels as the Heart-Shaped Meat Product (page 81), the Cube-Shaped Tennis Ball (page 49), and the Talking Toilet Paper Roll Holder (page 35).

Suddenly, the last eight years of my life made sense. My background in engineering, clowning, web development and stand-up comedy united behind a single purpose – I was uniquely equipped to ridicule nerds.

And that's how patentlysilly.com was born.

I've looked at every patent issued since then, more than half a million "advances" in technology. I've been amused, frightened and bored.

"Who are these freaks fiddling around in their basements in the middle of the night?" I asked myself at 4 a.m. while piecing together my website in my parents' spare bedroom.

I've learned that there are all different kinds of inventors. Some work for large companies, some work independently with few resources besides their ingenuity and passion, and others don't work so much as transcribe utterances from the spirit realm.

The only thing that unifies all of the inventors in this book is that their contributions to society have all been awarded a patent by the United States Patent and Trademark Office.[i] To receive a patent, an invention has to be deemed useful, unique and unobvious. Undoubtedly, to have one's work certified by a government agency as entirely new in the history of human civilization must inflate the ego.

…And that's where I come in to pop the bubble.

To be fair, most patents aren't that silly. Most of them are quite boring in fact. Only 0.26% of patents I see are chosen for patentlysilly.com (and even fewer for this book), and still many of these are serious scientific endeavours. There are two basic tests that I have. The invention must: (1) be explainable to the average person and (2) contain some element that inspires a funny thought.

Patents have a voyeuristic appeal. They are a window into the fears, problems and desires of our species. Terrorism, global warming, knobs – they all get addressed in quite imaginative ways. And then there are inventions that reveal the inner workings of some very narrow subcultures like "a meditation tool that also acts as a birdfeeder", a telephone that allows you to converse with a houseplant, and toothpick jewellery.

The phonograph, the aeroplane, the photocopier: all of these inventions were ridiculed when they were first invented. Perhaps laughter is the natural reaction to an idea that is entirely new. My goal is to be the first one to ridicule. Once we've laughed, perhaps the idea will sink in and slowly begin to change the world.

Thirty years from now, after you've had a nice workout on your cordless jump rope and eaten a nutritious meal of processed cow belches, you'll recline on your luxury, incinerating toilet, look at this book and laugh at how uncivilized we used to be.

DANIEL WRIGHT

i. The USPTO issues three types of patents:

1. Utility patents may be granted to anyone who invents or discovers any new and useful process, machine, article of manufacture, or composition of matter, or any new and useful improvement thereof;
2. Design patents may be granted to anyone who invents a new, original, and ornamental design for an article of manufacture; and
3. Plant patents may be granted to anyone who invents or discovers and asexually reproduces any distinct and new variety of plant.

Source: uspto.gov

Health
and Hygiene

Device for the Treatment of Hiccups
patent #: US 7062320

Is there a cure for hiccups that is not patently silly? Some people breathe into paper bags, others like a good scare, while the acrobatically inclined prefer to stand on their head and drink a glass of water. But the cures get even more extreme as the condition lingers. According to the inventor:

> Hiccups lasting up to 48 hours are classified as "bouts". Hiccups lasting longer than 48 hours are called "persistent". Those lasting longer than a month are called "intractable".

Hiccups lasting longer than a month! I would call that a living nightmare! At this point sufferers may resort to more extreme measures such as "inducing vomiting or applying pressure on the eyeballs."

Faced with the above options, you can see the incentive to innovate. This device is a metallic cup with electrodes that touch your cheek and temple. When the cup is full of water and you begin to drink, an electrical circuit is created, thus stimulating the vagus and phrenic nerves and "reliably interrupting the Hiccup Reflexive Arc." Nothing like a wholesome dose of electricity!

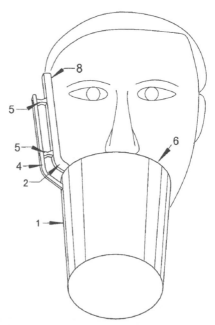

Burp Gas Filtering and Deodorizing Device

patent #: US 7070638

As instructed by the inventor:

> The user holds the upper end of the pen body to their lips and releases the suppressed burp. The filtered gas is then exhausted through the ports at the writing tip.

This invention hails from the genteel southern United States, where sharing the scent of one's partially digested food is apparently considered ill mannered. For refined gentlemen and women this portable gadget, conveniently disguised as a pen, contains a charcoal filter to contain the undesirable eructation.
> Belch squelched.

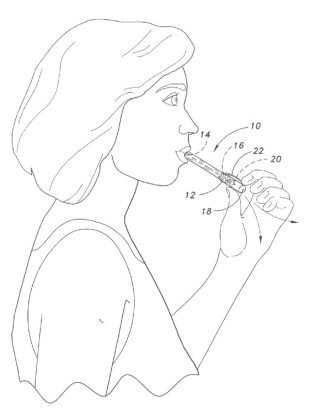

Method for Introducing a Powdered Substance Into a Nostril

patent #: US 6811543

A straw for introducing a powdered substance into a nostril? Surely this was invented in the 80s? (By the way, I love the use of the word "introducing" here. "Nostril, meet cocaine. Cocaine, nostril.")

This device, assigned to a drug delivery company, Direct-Haler A/S, enables you to blow a dose of whatever it is you need up your nose. Put one end in your mouth, one end in a nostril, and blow!

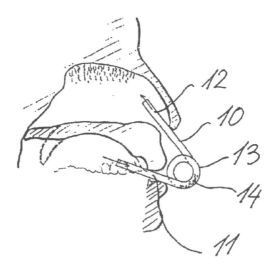

High-Pressure Water-Spray Device for Cleaning Teeth

patent #: US 6783505

This man looks like he lives a high-pressure lifestyle: he is bald; he squints; he has small, malformed ears. The poor fellow doesn't even have the time to commit to a thorough dental regimen. That's right, he is not a brusher. He is a hoser.

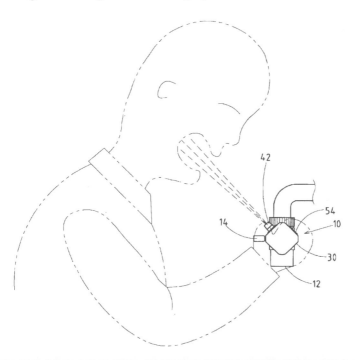

Novelty Bar of Soap Having Low Cost Electro-Mechanical Vibrating Assembly

patent #: US 6802819

Even soap has gotten dirty.

What is this obsession with turning every possible object into a vibrator? Apparently, it's the easiest way to get a patent: Take an object that already exists, make it vibrate, get a patent.

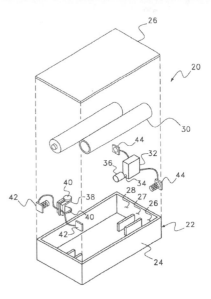

Illuminated Soap Bar with Sound

patent #: US 6746135

How much entertainment do we need in the shower?

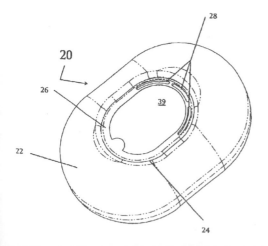

Simulated Disposable Foreskin for Training Surgical Procedure of Infant Circumcision

patent #: US 7080984

According to the inventor, the traditional approach to circumcision has been "See one, do one, teach one." Yikes! Whatever happened to "Practice makes perfect"? Circumcision isn't exactly like chopping firewood.

No doubt the sex toy industry has already pioneered the art of making realistic foreskinned faux-schlongs and will lend their expertise to doctors in training.

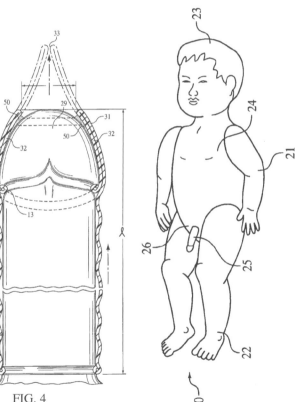

FIG. 4

Collapsible Walker

patent #: US D497845

Collapse… exactly what you don't want your walker to do.

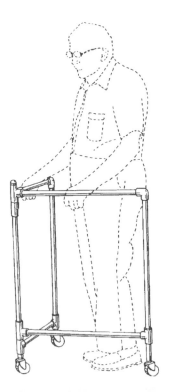

Backscratcher with a Telescopically Adjustable Shaft and with a Plurality of Screw-on Attachment End Pieces

patent #: US 6830552

Attachments include: a pointing hand, pointy teeth, a toothbrush, a mirror, a pen, a fork, a spoon, a Phillips screwdriver, a magnet, an alligator clip and a business card holder.

(Everything your back needs to be scratched, cleaned, groomed, written on, eaten off, opened, attached to an electrical circuit or introduced at a party.)

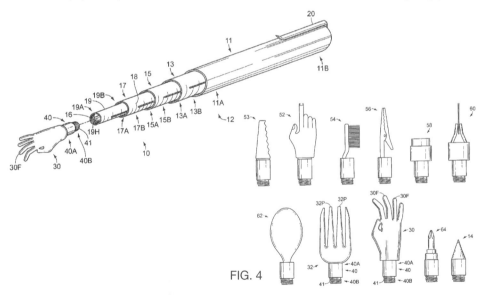

FIG. 4

Roller Tool for Applying Sunscreen Lotion to One's Own Back

patent #: US D497451

The skin care and house painting industries have finally joined forces.

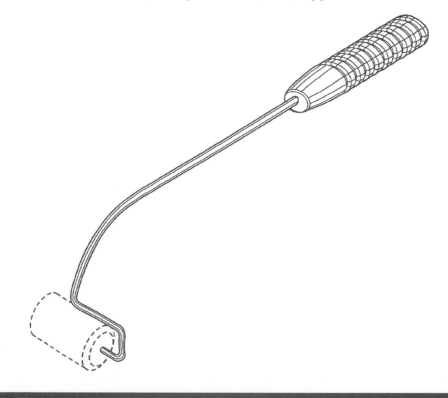

Sun Mask Towel

patent #: US 7051371

Ah, life without ozone, how my pale skin loves it.

From whence came this novel garment?

There is a need in the art for an easy to use, easy to carry form of sun protection that blocks harmful UV rays to the entire area of skin a user wishes to protect, while allowing a user to see, talk and breathe easily.

The need has been heard and it has been addressed! This thing looks like a cross between a turban, a bandana, and a Ku Klux Klan hood. Prevent sunburn and scare the crap out of people.

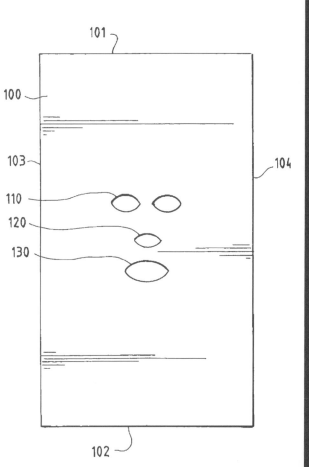

Arm Shades

patent #: US 6775844

The ozone layer is disappearing, which unfortunately means that some of us have to shield our bodies with ridiculous-looking accessories. This device is meant for people "driving with their window down… wearing short sleeves." The driver would be able to "experience air flow, while at the same time… virtually eliminate any chance of… receiving sun exposure." Crap for every occasion.

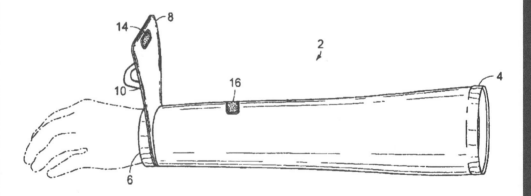

Male Genitalia Tanning Bed Shield

patent #: US D524945

Unfortunately for some people, this invention came just a little too late.

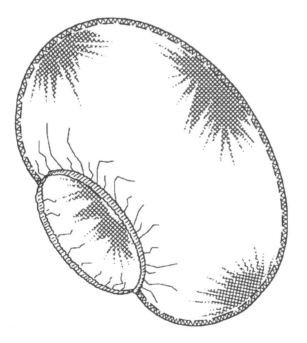

Expandable Vomit Container Assembly

patent #: US 7029463

Because you never quite know when you're finished.

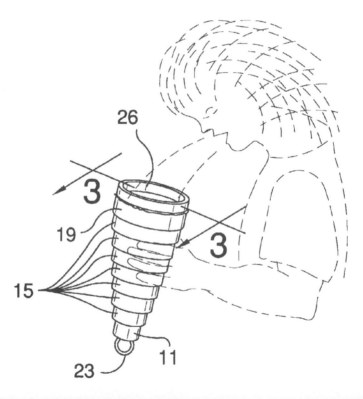

Human Waste Management Suit

patent #: US 6920646

Just the thought of all-out chemical warfare is enough to provoke multiple pant-soiling atrocities. But fear not, with this suit you can shit yourself silly and no one need know. Environmental hazard avoided, in your pants at least.

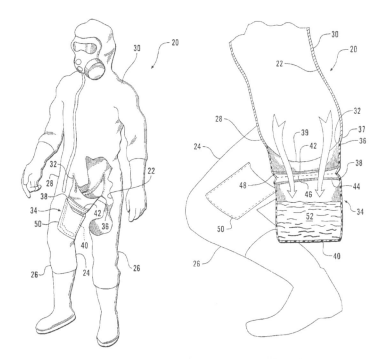

Self-Administered Two-Handled Probe for Treating Prostatitis

patent #: US 7077817

When threatened with cancer, one must be prepared to go to extremes. While some get chemo, a lucky few get this rectal joystick.

Sometimes a prostate just needs a rub (and not necessarily from a finger that's gone through four years of expensive medical schooling):

> The apparatus is employed by inserting the probe into the rectum from the rear of the patient and positioning the probe tip adjacent to the colon walls proximate the prostate. The patient then manipulates the probe using the handle grips on each side. They should be in a standing, bent over position, with a mirror placed on the floor between their feet to provide visual confirmation of the probe's location.

Presumably not to be done in public.

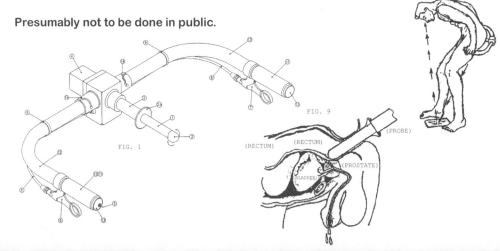

FIG. 1

FIG. 9

(PROBE)

(RECTUM)

(RECTUM)

(PROSTATE)

(BLADDER)

Micro Robot

patent #: US 6824508

Crikey, it's a robot that crawls up your anus. And it takes pictures! One can only pray that the accompanying illustration was not drawn to scale.

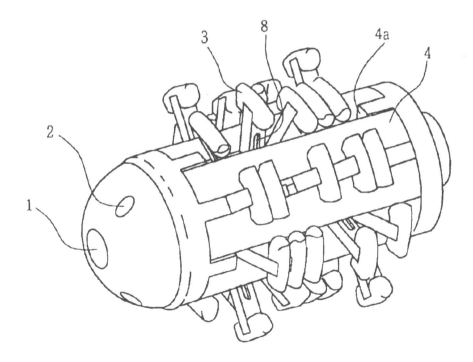

Sphincter Exerciser

patent #: US 6824500

At last, an improved piece of exercise equipment for those without bowel control. Step into the footholds and rotate your feet – you're going to have the fittest sphincter in town.

Forget Step class. Forget Spin class. It's time to Sphinc it up!

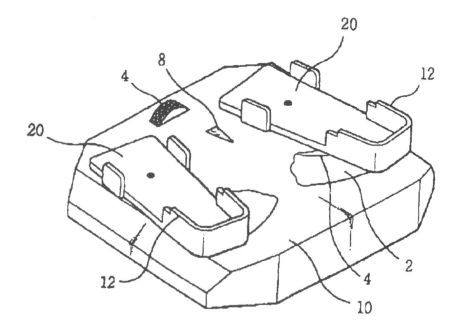

Flatulence Filter Seat Cushion for Absorbing Odour and Providing Sound Attenuation from an Anal Discharge of a Seated Individual

patent #: US 7073223

James Huza is an inventor who attacks the problem of smelly farts with a hardcore breakdown of the facts:

> "The average person produces two to three pints of gas daily, which leaves the body in the form of belching or flatus. On average, a flatus outburst for a normal person ranges from 10 to 20 occurrences per day... To minimize the effects of flatus a portable flatulence filter seat cushion... was invented."

According to Huza, it's perfect for "that special gift-giving occasion". Special gift-giving occasion? "Honey, you'll never guess what I got you for Valentine's Day!"

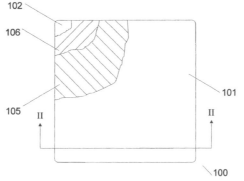

Luxury Toilet Having a Reclining Seat Back

patent #: US 7020907

According to the inventor, bathrooms "have evolved from rooms that simply provide a utilitarian function, to rooms that provide places of refuge from the everyday stresses of life." Baths and showers have kept up with trend, but unfortunately toilets have not. Hello, market opportunity.

The standard toilet was "not designed for comfort during long periods of sitting.... [T]he luxury toilet having the reclining back portion provides a comfortable and supportive place of rest for a user wishing to relax in the quiet environment of a bathroom."

Bliss while you piss.

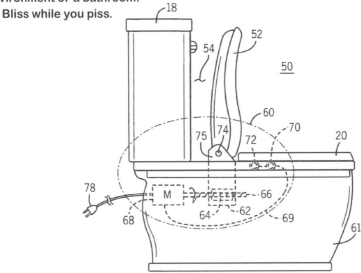

Incinerating Commode
patent #: US 6763528

For most people, excrement burning is a hobby that ends in youth. As a practical joke, you drop a burning bag of number two on a doorstep and ring the bell.

But for inventor James West, incinerating turds is a passion not easily extinguished. As he declares in his patent he has spent "over twenty years in devising improvements in incinerating commodes." He's not content to stop until he's blown the lid off the industry.

In the latest version, West's toilet separates the urine from the faeces, injects the stool with a combustible fluid, incinerates the matter with blow torches and then uses the urine to steam-clean the chamber.

Evacuate, incinerate, decontaminate. Who's next?

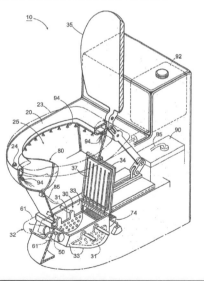

Lighted Traffic Sign Attached to Portable Restroom

patent #: US 6812856

You know those people at roadworks holding signs and directing traffic? This invention is for them. It includes a stool, a slot to put the sign in and a urinal.

See that arm sticking off to the side? That's the urinal. Right there in the open! Nice. Stop! Go! Stop! Aaaand shake.

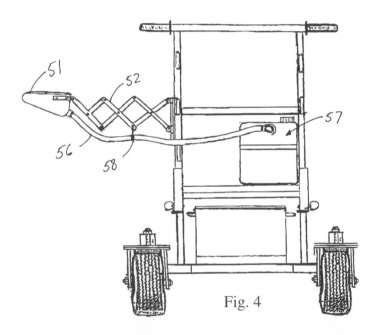

Fig. 4

Portable Toilet

patent #: US D500844

Perfect for garden parties and
fertilizing the lawn. Fold carefully.

Toilet Stool

patent #: US D529150

In case you need a lap to crap on.

Toilet Seat for Obese Persons

patent #: US D491650

Because one size does not always fit all.

FIG. 1

Portable Toilet

patent #: US D519645

Now you can literally go to "the can".

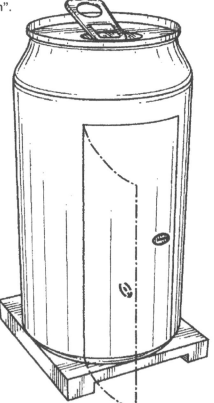

Talking Toilet Paper Roll Holder

patent #: US 6772975

What on Earth could it say? "Congratulations, one wipe wonder!" or "Still here?"
Or maybe it just scares the crap out of you.

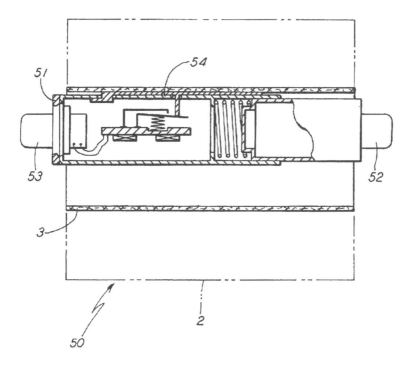

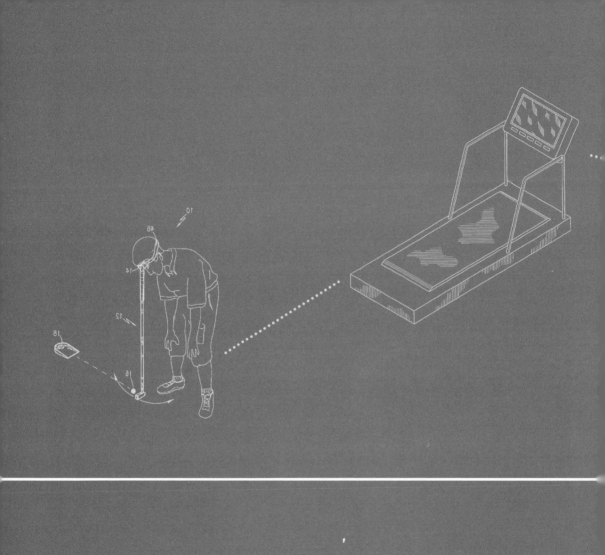

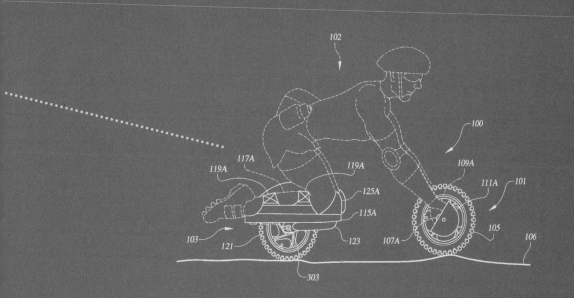

Recreation

Cordless Jump Rope

patent #: US 7037243

None of the rope, all of the jump.

This absurd invention "provides health enthusiasts all of the benefits of jumping rope with none of the disadvantages." If you really are that uncoordinated, might I suggest you try walking?

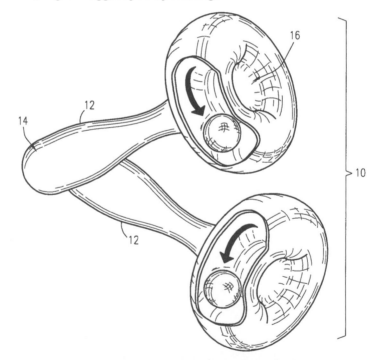

Abdominal Exercise Device for Use By a Person Sitting in an Automobile Seat and Doing Crunches

patent #: US 7083555

There can be little doubt that driving contributes to our obesity epidemic. Quite simply, we drive everywhere, burning petrol instead of fat. But now we don't need to decide between walking and driving; there's a compromise – exercise equipment has entered the automobile.

This invention allows you to tone your six-pack during your morning commute. Well, at least it's exercise (and presumably still faster than walking).

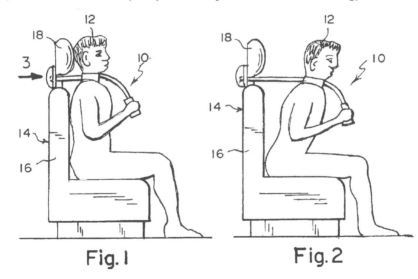

Fig. 1　　　　Fig. 2

Swim Machine
patent #: US 6764431

I thought this machine was just for people without access to a swimming pool, but the inventor suggests an additional market:

> The device allows users to "swim" in the privacy of one's own home, thereby avoiding the embarrassment that some individuals have with being seen by others in form fitting swimwear.

And for keeping them indoors, we thank you!

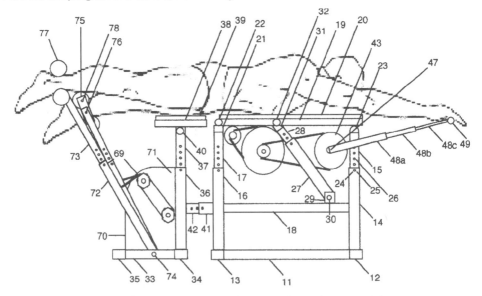

Wind-Assisted Bicycle

patent #: US 6880844

Contrary to just about every development in bicycle technology over the last hundred years, this bicycle adds wind resistance in its attempt to harness Mother Nature's exhale. What happens when the wind blows against you? (I'll trust the inventor thought this one through.) You may not be able to weave in and out of traffic, but you will be able to plough through pedestrians.

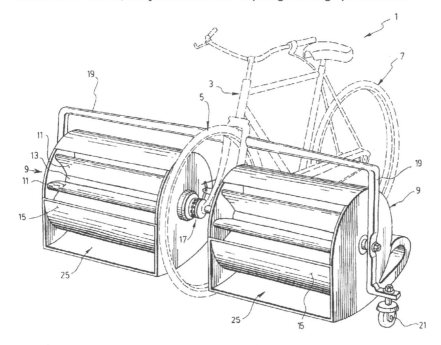

Hip Hop Aerobic Exercise Doll

patent #: US 7128691

I can't decide which is odder, doing hip-hop aerobics with a robotic doll or incorporating VHS tapes into twenty-first-century technology.

As the video plays this doll gets jiggy to the soundtrack. Obese children will presumably be inspired to shake their bloated, candy-fed behinds along with this Caucasian-looking, hip hop-dancing automaton. According to the inventor, this groovy golem "will promote better health in the youth", "significantly reduce medical costs associated with overweight people", and, thankfully, "be made available with designer clothing".

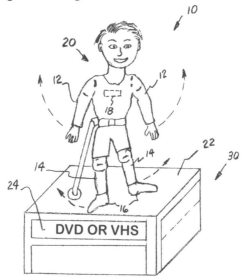

Intragastric Prosthesis for the Treatment of Morbid Obesity

patent #: US 6755869

What does dietary science have to teach us this time? Any random object you put in your stomach will help you lose weight, except for food.

This new procedure of the Boston Scientific Corporation involves dropping a bio-absorbable ball into the stomach to create that "just had two Double Whoppers" feeling.

Sponge-ball soup anyone?

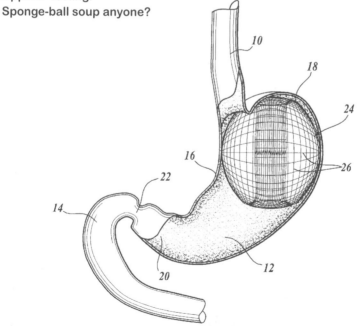

Golf Club

patent #: US 6872148

Get a few extra yards in your drive by detonating an explosive charge (seriously)! Golfers are so desperate to get a competitive advantage on the fairway that some are considering using the boom-boom powder.

A cartridge is mounted in the head of the golf club. When you strike the ball, the propelling charge is detonated to give your drive an extra boost.

Fore? More like .44! Now I know why golf courses have bunkers.

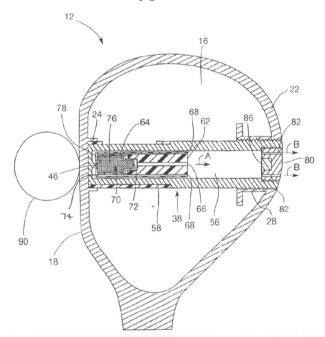

Weed Cutting Golf Club

patent #: US 6988954

This sly club comes in handy when you've landed in the rough. No need to bogey the hole just because you're surrounded by two-foot-high grass – buzz your way to a clear shot!

But inventors John Buell and Troy Nowell see their gas-powered, weed-whacking wood as more than the latest must-have accessory: it's a humble contribution towards world peace. It is "a weed cutting golf club for relief of stress" that can "lighten the mood and decrease stress levels in order to provide a more relaxing and enjoyable atmosphere".

Rev up and chill out.

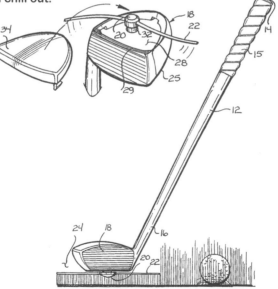

Telescopic Putter Mounted to Headband
patent #: US 6814671

It's a putter that you strap to your head. Admittedly, if this had been sensitively invented to allow amputees to pursue their passion for golfing, I think we'd all take our hats off to the inventor. But judging by the fact that his illustration depicts what looks like a perfectly able-bodied male (albeit wearing three-quarter length combat trousers), it's probably safe to assume he's insane.

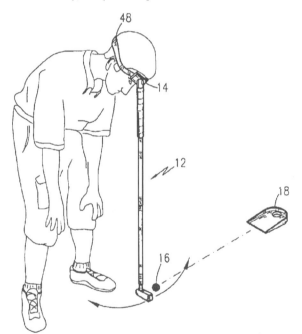

Golf Exercise Treadmill

patent #: US D496699

This treadmill design is for "golf exercise" only. What's the difference between "golf exercise" and walking? I have no idea. Maybe you're supposed to carry your golf clubs? It's okay to light a cigar after 100 yards? You wear plaid spandex?

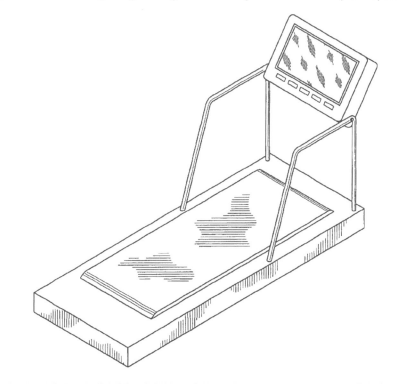

No-Crap Craps:
Crapless Craps Done Right
patent #: US 7134660

Wheel out the guillotine, 'cause this game's getting decrapitated! *Merde* she wrote!

Finally, someone's done it right! Let me tell you, crapless craps done wrong, is, well, just plain crap. I'm not much of a gambling man, but something tells me that if you take the crap out of craps, you don't have much left.

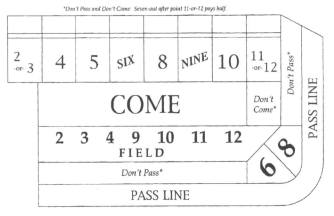

Besides having the crappiest name for a patent I've ever seen (next to the "Collapsible Walker"), this invention has the honour of being the latest in a series of attempts to cut the crap from the popular dice game.

"Craps" refers to a losing result (a 2, 3, or 12) on your very first roll of the dice, known as the "come out". There have been several attempts to remove this nightmare moment from the game, all with trademarked names: Crapless Craps; Never Ever Craps; and now, No-Crap Craps. How many ways can you scrap the crap? Now excuse me while I go wash my hands.

Cube-Shaped Tennis Ball

patent #: US D498801

Picasso does Wimbledon.

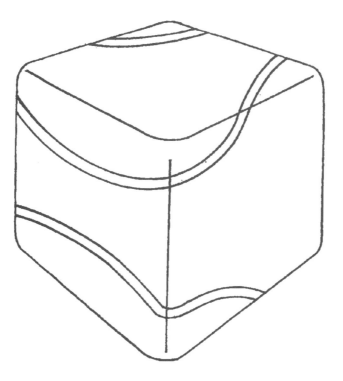

Mermaid Fish Lure

patent #: US D491623

Fish are finicky creatures. You never know what they're going to be in the mood for – a worm, a slug, or a hot piece of ass straight out of Greek mythology.

Fishing Lure

patent #: US D496090

I don't understand these fishing lures. This one looks like an S&M Ken doll.

Why the human form? Is the idea to bait the fish with some kind of Shakespearean revenge fantasy? As if there's some poor trout down there soliloquizing, "If you hook us, do we not bleed? And if you wrong us, shall we not revenge?" Demanding a pound of human flesh just as the lure comes down...

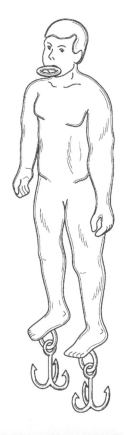

Fishing Rod with Gun Features

patent #: US D523921

Rubbish lures not working? Sometimes you run out of patience…

Hunter's Chair

patent #: US 6755466

From what I've gathered sifting through patents, hunting is a waiting game. You head out to the woods, set yourself up behind a blind, and then sit and wait (and drink!)... for hours... days... however long it takes for an animal to wander into range.

Hunting does have its dangers – one being lower back pain from all of that sitting and waiting. Enter US Patent #6755466. From now on, a hunter's essentials include guns, ammo, and a little lumbar support.

What's the difference between this and an ordinary office chair? Easy now, you little skeptic, don't you see the camouflage?

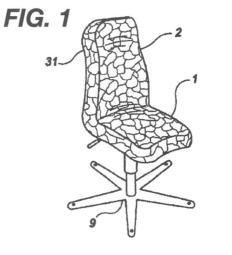

FIG. 1

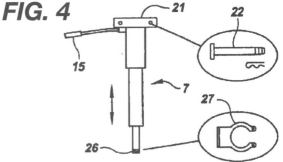

FIG. 4

SUV Tent

patent #: US D503143

Why tire yourself hiking when you can turn on your portable TV and watch The Discovery Channel? Why search the woods for kindling when you can roast marshmallows over the engine block? Why be kept up all night by strange noises when you can get the quality sleep that only carbon monoxide can provide?

Wing Device for Sporting Activities

patent #: US 7097134

There's no danger of the feathers melting with this wing device – it's intended for the icy cold realms of the ski slope. The inventor aims considerably lower than Icarus, using the wing-flapping motion "to help propel the user on flat ground". While the device does provide lift, it can also be used for duller purposes such as braking and turning. And making you look silly.

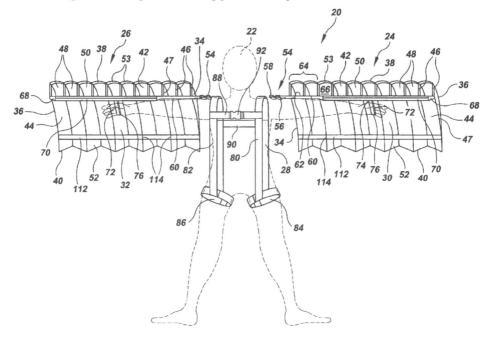

Body-Connected Bike

patent #: US 6805657

Man and machine merge in this crazy invention from Oklahoma. Who needs a
bike frame, when you can be the bike? Inventor Justin W. Trenary seeks to create
a new X-game in the category of dangerous things you can do with gravity.
According to Trenary:

> Downhill vehicle riding has constantly been a popular activity for sport,
> competition and fitness… Many individuals look for new equipment and
> methods in which to display quickness, strength, physical stamina and
> good reflexes.

Your legs strap in to the back portion, while your hands grab the front axle.
Hey, at least if you fall, you won't fall far…

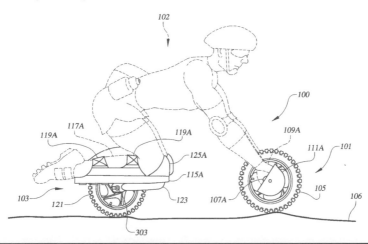

Combination Powered Parachute and Motorcycle

patent #: US 6877690

Hells Angels don't earn their wings, they build them. Who has the time to take off eyebrow rings and studded collars to get past airport security? Screw it! There's got to be some way to get a Harley to fly. *Voilà*.

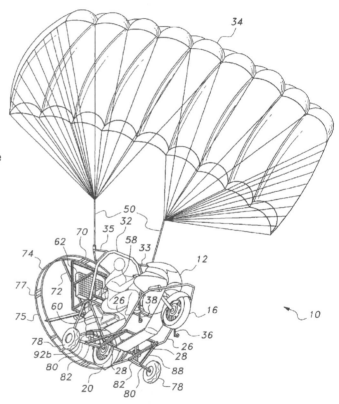

Photographing Game Machine

patent #: US 6832954

Steady. Focus. Shoot!

Do you dream of being a sports photographer, but can't get front-row seats? Do you yearn to be a fashion photographer, but are scared of women? Do you just want to hold a camera in your hand, but can't afford one? Save your pennies for NAMCO's Photographing Game Machine and snap away.

Never has a video game been further away from the excitement.

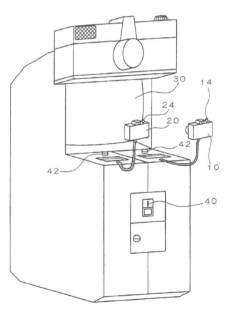

Method and Apparatus for Identifying a Winner in a Bingo Game

patent #: US 6755739

"Method and apparatus for identifying a winner in a bingo game"?

Okay… deep, relaxing breath in… deep, relaxing breath out. *Look for the person jumping up and down yelling "Bingo!"* No special "Method" or "Apparatus" needed!

What happened to the days when yelling the name-o of the game-o was all you needed to do to claim-o victory? As I recall, hearing some imbecile (myself included) scream in ecstasy after successfully determining the intersection of letter and number was the most interesting part of the game. But my days of bingo were a long time ago… before online gambling, before "Power Bingo," before a company named Bingo Innovation Software could hope to have a successful business model…

PATTERN MATCHING ARRAY   500

B	I	N	G	O
X				X
	X		X	
		X		
	X		X	
X				X

Mirror Checkers/Chess

patent #: US 7017906

There's something creepy about these twins playing their mirror chess. They freak me out, like those albino twins from *The Matrix: Reloaded*. Not only are they playing mirror chess, but they're practically mirror images of each other: They have the same posture, identical cheek scars... even their shirts wrinkle in the same way!

And notice that they are completely enraptured by the game, but there aren't even any pieces on the board. Do you think they are playing telepathically with imaginary pieces? Do you think they know that I am writing about them? Or that you are reading about them? I've got the spooky feeling that they're about to twist their necks and glare at us... *Quick, turn the page!*

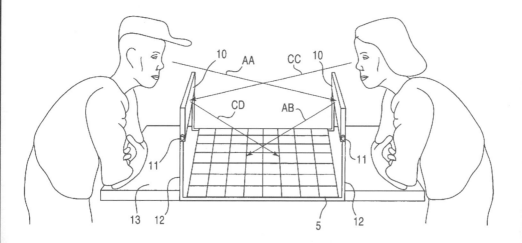

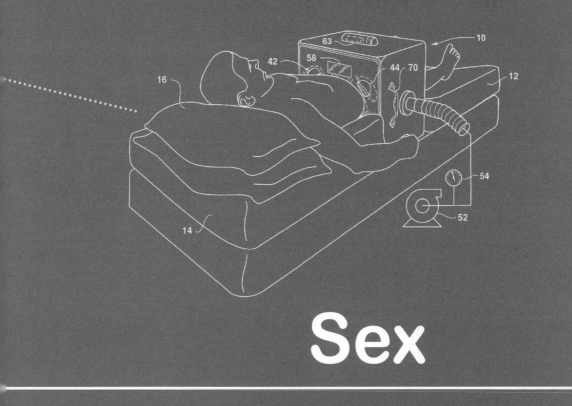

Sex

Penile Volumetric Measuring Device
patent #: US 7147609

Penis size: for too long (puns are inevitable when discussing the subject), it has escaped the rigorous analysis of modern science and has been left prone to self-serving exaggeration. Thankfully, one fearless inventor has arrived to clear the field of biased pseudo-science.

Just 22 short centuries since Archimedes first shouted "*Eureka!*" from his bathtub, inventor Jason Turner has applied the same techniques of fluid displacement to accurately measure the one-eyed trouser snake.

Of course, scientific breakthroughs are often met with fierce resistance: knowledge is power, yes. But the truth (if small enough) can hurt.

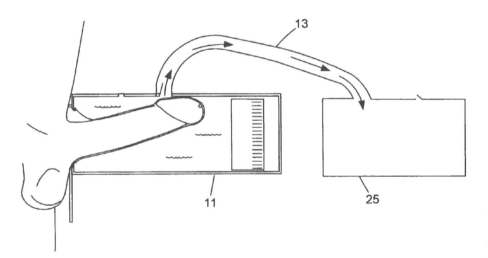

Condom with Inflatable Portion

patent #: US
6895967

The title and picture pretty much say it all –
this rubber provides extra girth when you need it. A well placed squeeze can do wonders. This distinctly unromantic jimmy hat can be "repetitively inflated and deflated
at desired times", much like a man's ego when he's told, "Yes, I want
to have sex, but where's your penis?"

I shouldn't knock it until I've tried it, but it's not a preferred
way of "getting blown". Common sense will
tell you that balloons and pricks are best
kept separate.

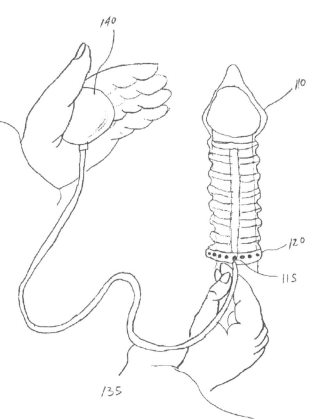

Magnetic Condom

patent #: US 6863070

This condom provides "static magnetic field therapy", supposedly increasing blood flow to the region. The magnetic cock ring must already be patented.

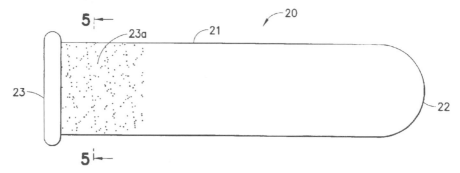

Novelty Condom

patent #: US D525357

Although the molestation of inflatable dolphins is probably more common, there are apparently other fetishists who want to be penetrated by a dolphin. Make sure you seal the blowhole first!

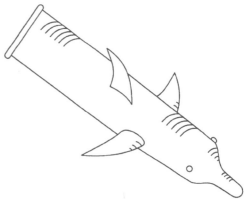

Male Prophylactic Garment

patent #: US D523140

The world's most successful contraceptive. You'll never get laid wearing one.

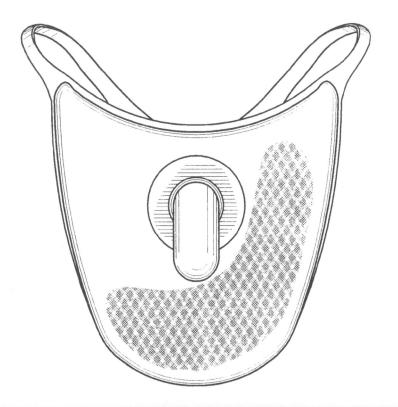

Lap Dance Liner

patent #: US RE39371

It is said that Thomas Edison's laboratory went through over 100,000 failed prototypes for each successful invention. One can only hope that in the quest for his perfect liner, Wesley K. Johnson went through as many lap dances.

I don't think this invention needs much explanation, but one sentence in this patent surprised me. The inventor points out that the pouch "captures fluids released prior to, and during the lap dance act." *Prior* to? Now that's excitable!

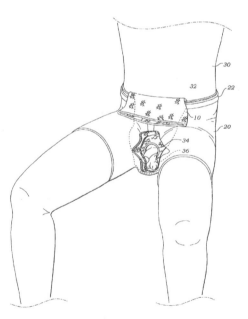

Hinging Breast Implant

patent #: US 6875233

Do you want breast implants, but aren't sure which size to get? Then maybe a hinging implant is what you need.

This implant can be resized at any time – like a bicycle tyre! A flexible bladder acts as a bellows to let you expand or contract your breasts to whatever size suits your fancy. The valve on the side stays just beneath the surface of your skin, so you can change the size and firmness with only a little minor surgery.

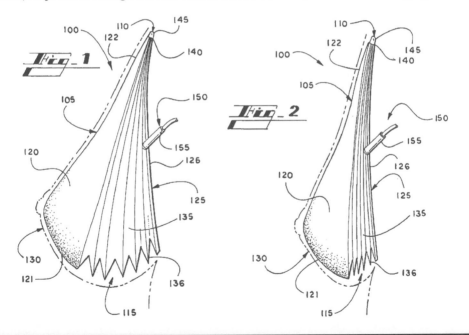

Pelvic Extension Frame

patent #: US 7029428

What exactly is a "sexy walk"? According to the inventor, no one really knows for sure, "its definition is analogous to the definition of pornography – 'I know it when I see it.'"

This frame helps by "visually amplifying the motions of the pelvis, [so that] an individual can be trained to exaggerate the movement of the pelvis and thereby develop a 'sexy' walk." So sexy it will knock over the furniture.

And good luck, guy in the patent illustration. Practise your walk, pay for the sex change, and you'll have what it takes to become Britain's Next Top Model.

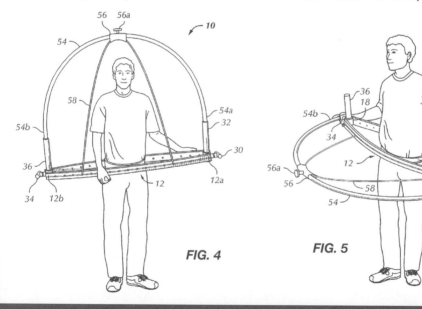

FIG. 4

FIG. 5

Method of Using a Water Pipe

patent #: US 7122000

I've heard of snorting coke off a stripper's tits, but taking a bong hit out of her vagina?

This "water pipe providing sexual stimulation" seems to be just too depraved to be true. With inventions like this, I find it best to let the patent do the talking:

> The lower end cooperates[!] with the wall of the vagina to form a reservoir holding water in the lower end and the vagina. Suction applied at the exit port draws air through the stem to bubble through the water reservoir and generate stimulatory vibrations transmitted to the vagina. Optionally, a bowl holding combustible material communicates with the stem such that smoke bubbles through the water reservoir to simultaneously filter and cool the smoke and generate stimulatory vibrations.

Maybe the bubbling is pleasurable, but pleasurable enough to allow bong water in your vagina? Perhaps the only thing not surprising about this patent is that comes from Las Vegas. Hopefully, it will stay there.

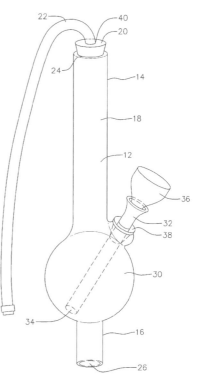

Automated Detection of Pornographic Images

patent #: US 6751348

Pornography is a controversial subject – some people hate it, some people love it. This invention is for both groups of people. Seek or avoid – the choice is yours!

It uses colour and texture to determine if an image contains skin. From there it moves on to locate a face, genitalia, and even "an erotic position" (as demonstrated by this no-nippled, claw-footed damsel).

The female form has never been so thoroughly objectified.

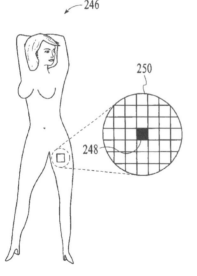

246

250

248

$$V = \frac{\sum_t^P \sqrt{colour^2}}{P}$$

V is variance
P is number of pixels

$$colour^2 = (L - mean\ L)^2 + (a - mean\ a)^2 + (b - mean\ b)^2$$

$$mean\ L = \frac{\sum_l^P L}{P} \qquad mean\ a = \frac{\sum_l^P a}{P}$$

$$mean\ b = \frac{\sum_l^P b}{P}$$

$V \geq 10 \rightarrow$ not skin

$V < 10 \rightarrow$ skin

Internal Implement Allotropy Sexual Aid Utensil Universal-DISK

patent #: US 7131444

You might not have known such standards existed, but this somewhat awkwardly titled patent sets "a new standard for internal personal prevention worn in the female vagina". It is an anti-rape device, quite admirable in its thoroughness. Worn inside the vagina like a tampon, the invention delivers a "sharp, non-lethal pain to the head of the penis" of any would-be rapist. The hollow cavity is designed to collect evidence, ensuring that the man with the mangled willy is whisked straight off to prison for a very long time.

Rape? Sharp penis pain? Convictions? How is this a *Patently Silly* invention? Because, as the inventor acknowledges:

> Men considering rape, after this invention becomes known, will hopefully not attempt it, with the dread that any women *[sic]* could be wearing this…

Just the idea of it is enough – it doesn't even need to become a product to be effective. So help me spread the word!

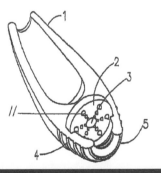

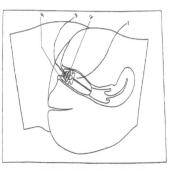

Method of Shared Erotic Experience and Facilities for Same

patent #: US 6805663

Lock yourself in your private pod, lie back in your (hopefully) sanitized hot-tub and relax to the moans of your neighbours.

Is this life in a poorly constructed apartment building? Nope, it's orgy-lite.

Inspired by the success of Japanese "Love Hotels", which cater to the needs of twenty-somethings still living at home, pod loving is a half-rung up the respectability ladder from a peep-show booth. Will the pods catch on? The inventor must share the faith of Kevin Costner's character in *Field of Dreams*: if you build it, they will come…

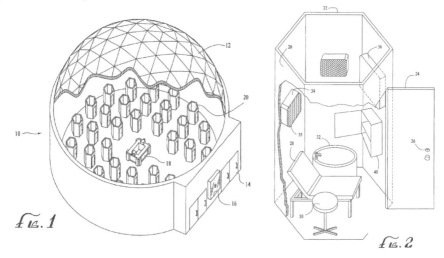

Fig. 1

Fig. 2

Electrode Apparatus for Stimulating Penile, Urethral, and Anal Tissue

patent #: US 6785577

Love can be electrifying. But what do you do when your loving spark is absent?
Do you sit there and sulk? Cheat on your partner? No. You empower yourself.

But is this invention really new? I could swear I once saw an old wood-block
print of Benjamin Franklin wearing one of these in a thunderstorm.

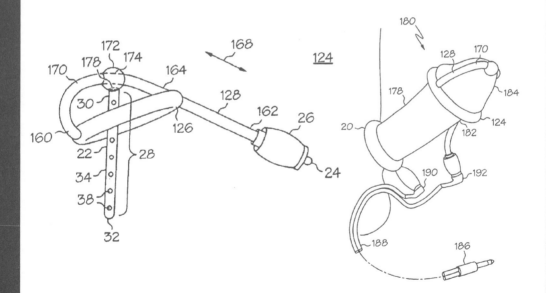

Apparatus and Method to Assist in the Diagnosis of Premature Ejaculation

patent #: US 6814695

This seems like an overly complicated method of diagnosing an easily identified problem. Ask any woman: if she's not satisfied yet, it's premature.

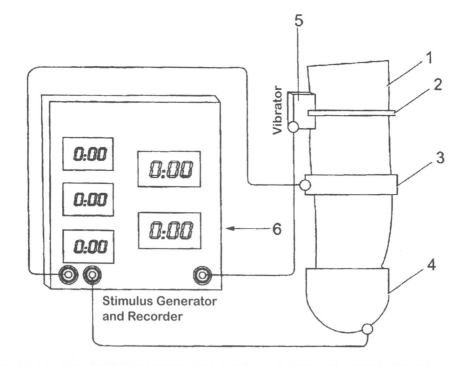

Spinal Cord Stimulation as a Therapy for Sexual Dysfunction

patent #: US 6862479

It's a sign of a great society when someone incapable of getting an erection without electrocuting their spinal column can still get laid.

This boner-inducing patent is assigned to California-based Advanced Bionics Corporation. A bionic erection? Now that's a pick-up line!

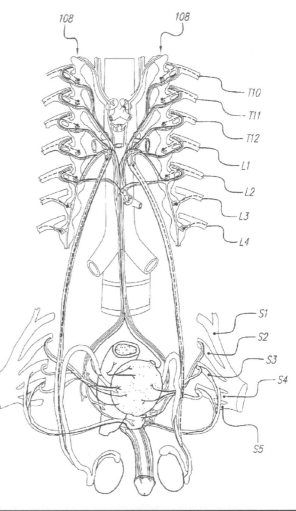

Male Impotence Prosthesis Apparatus with Wireless Energy Supply

patent #: US 7011624

Filed on Valentine's Day 2001, this invention may one day make the erectionally-challenged as stiff as Cupid's arrow.

Implanted in the corpora cavernosa (a.k.a. the shaft), it consists of a hydraulic pump connected to a reservoir. An external power source wirelessly activates the pump, which draws fluid from the reservoir to fill up the penis. It's a hands-free hard-on!

And when the job is done, you just put it in reverse and you're back to your usual, flaccid self.

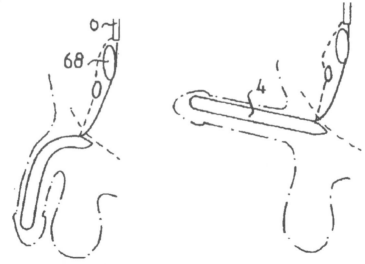

Device for Treating Erectile Dysfunction
patent #: US 6905459

A high-tech erection machine? Tell me more, Mr Inventor: "Some of the reports indicate that ejaculation and orgasm three times a week is healthful."

If an orgasm three times a week is "healthful", then I'm an organic watercress and tofu salad. Basically, you clamber into this metal case, manually stimulate yourself, let the vacuum chamber suck all the blood into your schlong, then clamber out and put your new-found boner to good use.

So you wank, turn on a vacuum, and then just wank again? Or tie off your penis like a piece of balloon sculpture and have sex? Perhaps there's something here I'm not getting. Perhaps I am just too young to play with such toys.

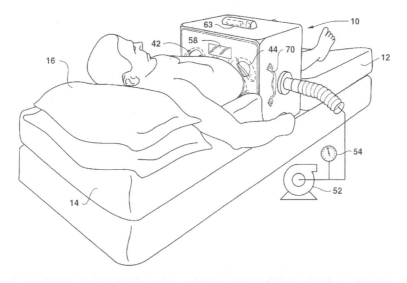

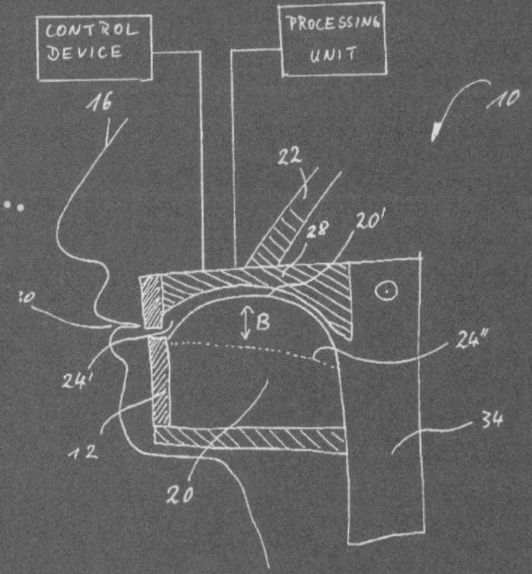

CONTROL
DEVICE

PROCESSING
UNIT

16

22

28

20'

10

24'

12

20

B

24"

34

Food
and Drink

Nutcracker

patent #: US D494820

Nothing busts a nut better than a strong pair of thighs.

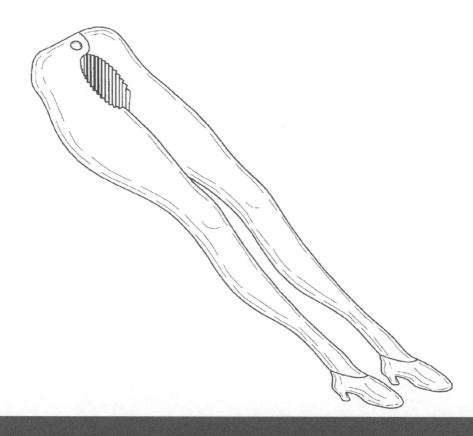

Heart Shaped Meat Product

patent #: US D490211

Even a vegan would blush if you grilled her up one of these romantic beef slabs. Well done, Romeo, well done!

Method for Producing Tissue Engineered Meat for Consumption

patent #: US 6835390

Get all the meat with none of the killing. This "tissue engineered meat product" is grown in the lab!

Muscle cells grow on a three-dimensional support structure to provide the naturally grown flavour and texture you desire. A full menu of meats is promised, including buffalo, alligator and frog's legs. And don't worry, gristle lovers, the inventor promises that your steak can be grown with "fat cells or cartilage"!

This may seem like a patently evil invention at first, but the inventor defends his morality. With most of the world's grain being used to feed animals, rainforests being cut down for grazing, overfishing and countless diseases spreading to humans through the food chain, we must find a less wasteful and less dangerous source of food. Growing meat in a petri dish doesn't seem so awful next to 50,000 people a day dying of starvation – nor, come to think of it, does vegetarianism.

If this ever reaches the market, it will be a brave new bite for mankind.

Heart Shaped Cheese Slice

patent #: US D491711

Top off your "Heart Shaped Meat Product" with this patented "Heart Shaped Cheese Slice"!

Orienting and Sorting Device for Corn Dogs

patent #: US 6889821

For people who believe that the hot dog is best enjoyed battered in corn meal and shoved on the end of a stick, this image of spiralling corn dogs should fuel a few nights of high-sodium dreams.

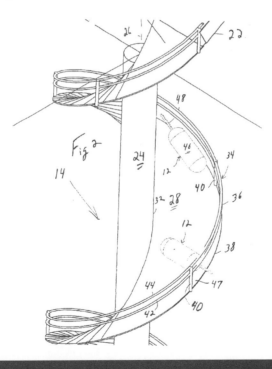

Pizza Preparation and Delivery Method and Unit

patent #: US 6858243

Is that pizza dough being tossed through the sun-roof? Your order will never be late again with this mobile pizza assault vehicle. The pizza can now be baked on the way to your house. Just keep one hand on the wheel, mate!

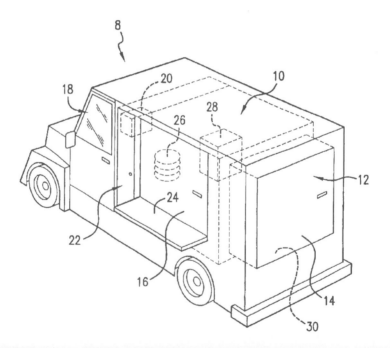

Writing and Candy Utensil

patent #: US 6984087

"A writing & candy utensil for giving a user something sweet to chew on rather than the end of the writing utensil."

Because one bad habit deserves another...

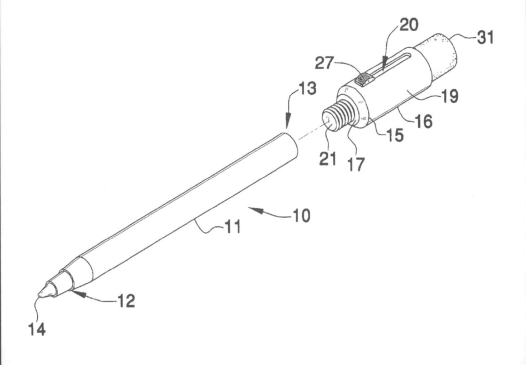

Combination Lollipop, Drinking Straw
patent #: US D491336

If you feel yourself slipping into a diabetic coma, stick one of these in your favourite soft drink for a powerful sugar-intake cocktail.

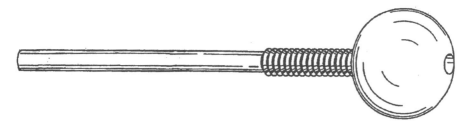

Alcoholic Beverages
Derived from Animal Extract
patent #: US 7037541

Inventor Kineo Okada of Tokyo has given you a new reason to raise your glass – there's a whole new breed of booze on its way to market and it's made of animals!

Okada is the President of Ariake Japan Company, whose service mark is "The Fine Flavours of Nature". Fine indeed! I can't wait to swirl my glass and enjoy an aromatic blend of "beef, pork, mutton, chicken, duck and turkey." So long, Burger King, this guy knows how to treat a carnivore.

Now, just how bloody do you like your Bloody Mary?

Combined Coconut-Shaped Drink Container and Coin Bank

patent #: US D505832

Because nothing spices up a Piña Colada like a fistful of germ-ridden spare change fished from the depths of your pocket…

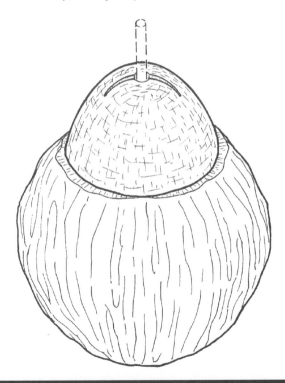

Simulated Wedding Cake

patent #: US 7021465

A "Simulated Wedding Cake"? How does one "invent" a simulation? Isn't a simulation, by definition, a copy? And by simulating a wedding cake, wouldn't one risk starting a revolution? For goodness sake they're at a wedding, let them eat cake!

But let us not judge too quickly. What sensual delights does such a sim-cake contain? Let me taunt your salivary glands with a description from the patent:

> [A] plurality of stackable layers oriented in a substantially vertical manner… having a centrally disposed longitudinal axis extending therethrough.

Geometrically delicious. Lick my longitudinal axis, Nigella Lawson!

This sim-cake is really a way to distribute capsules of confetti to throw over the newlyweds during their exit. Apparently slicing the cake is too difficult and time-consuming.

Most likely, the marriage isn't going to last too long, anyway. Don't waste precious time cutting a cake!

Device for Determining and Characterizing Noises Generated By Mastication of Food

patent #: US 6792324

As we've all learned from television commercials, crispiness is a coveted property in snack foods – perhaps the highest of virtues. So how do food companies test the crunch factor?

In this invention, an artificial head does the chewing while multiple microphones pick up the air-conducted and bone-conducted sounds. All in the name of crisps... er... I mean science.

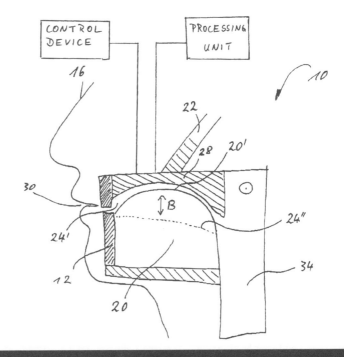

Timed Drinking Vessel

patent #: US 6747918

One of the inventors of this vessel hails from Milwaukee, Wisconsin, the spiritual homeland of American beer. The digital timer on the front helps make sure that you never drink too fast (or too slow) again. Cheers!

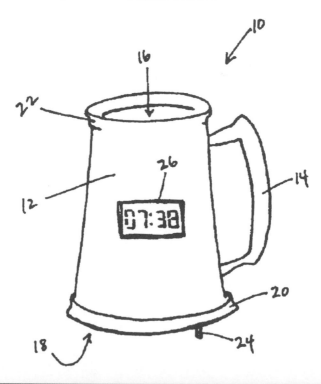

Cane

patent #: US 6745785

This cane has not one, not two, but three flasks built into it – all for storing alcohol and mixers. As the inventor points out, "Aficionados of fine wines and liquors often find themselves in locations lacking in such drink." This thing will help you get drunk and stay upright!

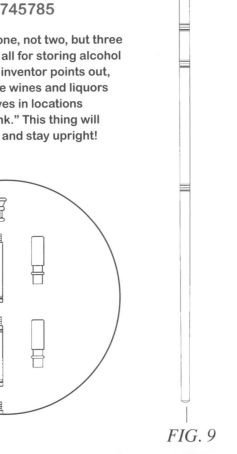

FIG. 9   FIG. 10

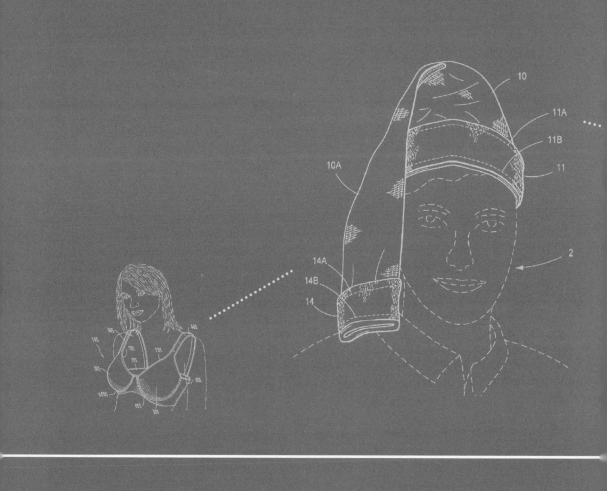

Clothing and Accessories

Article of Clothing with a Novel Attachment Means

patent #: US 6832983

Tired of that thong creeping up your bum? Your best solution might be to jam it in further. This invention holds your clothes in place by snapping them onto a bulb that is inserted into your vagina and/or rectum.

In one version of the suit you squeeze the air out of the bulb, insert it in your chosen orifice and then let it fill back with air to create a watertight seal. If you're worried about pickpockets on the beach, the bulb has enough room for "a key, ID, and some parking meter change"!

These "minimalist bathing suits" are also safer than traditional suits. As the inventor points out, you don't have to lift a leg to get them on or off, "allowing one to minimize the risk of falling over." Safety before modesty!

The female versions come in three sizes: Lolita, Regular, and M.I.L.F.

A young woman or girl might need a very small extension, whereas a woman who is sexually active might need a larger one, and a woman who has had several children might need a larger one still.

Vibrating bulbs are optional.

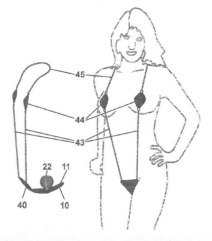

Optical Illusion Wear

patent #: US 7107621

There are many ways to obtain a slimmer figure: exercise, dieting, amphetamines. But sometimes, even popping pills is just too much work. Sometimes a lady just wants to create a "false or deceptive visual impression" without the hassle. Enter optical illusion wear. There's nothing wrong with manipulating someone's cognitive processes, is there? It's the oldest trick in the book! Think of it as beer goggles without the drinking.

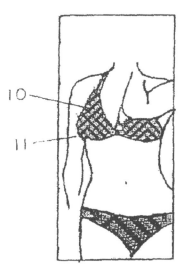

Figure 8 – Enlarging

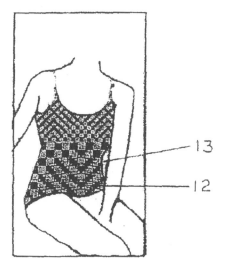

Figure 9 – Slimming

Garments Having Edible Components and Methods for Making Same

patent #: US 6872119

Picture the scene: it's your third date, you've invited her in for coffee, you take her up to your bedroom, you start to slowly nibble her clothes off. First you chew off her liquorice cagoule, then you gnaw away at her high heels. Eventually, you reveal her sexy lingerie; you're about to go in for the kill…

Then your teeth collapse and your face explodes because you've just eaten twice your recommended annual allowance of sugar.

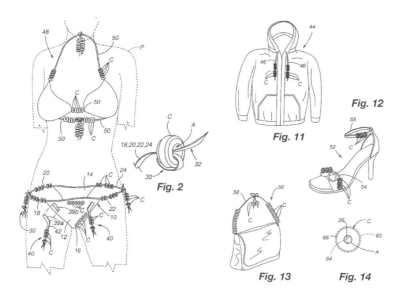

Fig. 2

Fig. 11

Fig. 12

Fig. 13

Fig. 14

Abdominal Support

patent #: US 6846220

Designed for pregnant women, this belly bra patent was carefully worded to include use by the obese – because hey, they're the bigger market.

My only complaint: where's the beer holder?

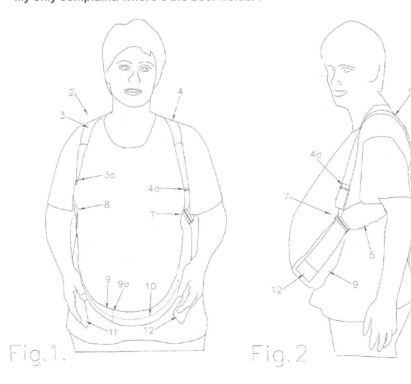

Fig.1.   Fig.2

Air Filled Brassiere

patent #: US 6811463

Get ready to inflate your bust ladies, it's bubble wrap for breasts! Gentlemen, be careful pinning on that brooch.

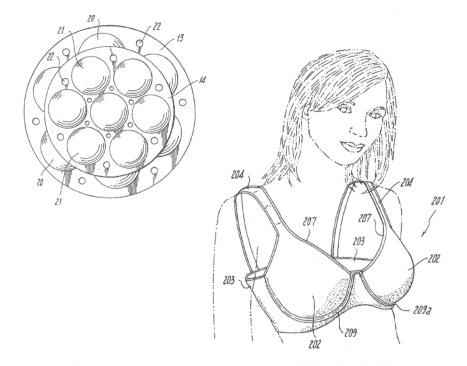

Pants with One or More Zippers on the Rear Thereof

patent #: US 6789269

Let's face it, we've pushed the limits of butt-cheek exposure with trousers in their current form. Luckily, fashion evolves quickly. These pants have zippers carefully designed to slyly reveal one cheek at a time. Didn't Prince invent these?

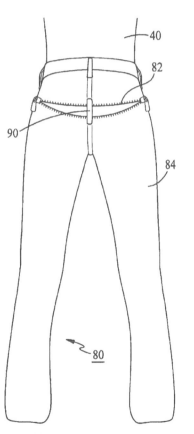

Jumpsuit for a Woman and Method of Use

patent #: US 6944883

Parachuting femmes will no doubt rejoice to finally have a jumpsuit designed for a woman's anatomical needs. Could there be anything more awkward than struggling to take a leak in a male's jumpsuit while approaching the earth at terminal velocity?

And could this be the first lesbian in a patent illustration? I'm not saying you can judge a person's sexuality by their appearance, but this lady sure bears a resemblance to a former gym teacher of mine, Ms. Butch Van Straponheimer.

In a steamy series of illustrations demonstrating the garment, this line-drawn vixen proves she's tough, she's sexy and she's not afraid to bare her arse to the US Patent Office.

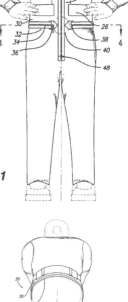

FIG. 1

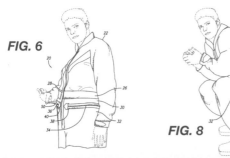

FIG. 6

FIG. 8

Cap with Integral Bottle Opener

patent #: US D503516

The "Cap with Integral Bottle Opener" is easily the most requested item on the *Patently Silly* website. Personally, I find the bigger leaps of invention more compelling, but I guess an open beer is what society really needs.

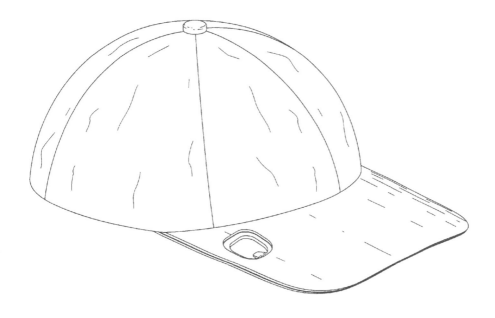

Multi-Purpose Headgear

patent #: US 6889797

Carry beer, drown out the screams of everyone around you, *and* warn traffic after you've passed out in the car park? What more could a sports fan want from a hat? You want to fill it with presents on Christmas morning? *It does that, too!*

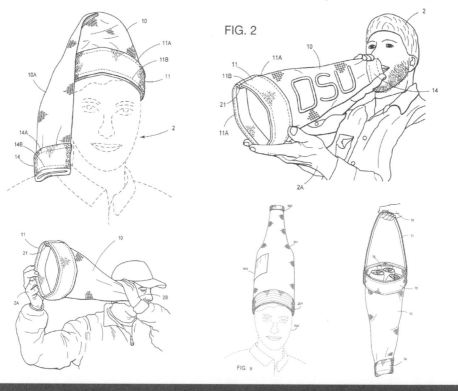

Novelty Hat

patent #: US D502588

WARNING: People wearing tyre hats may attract tyre irons.

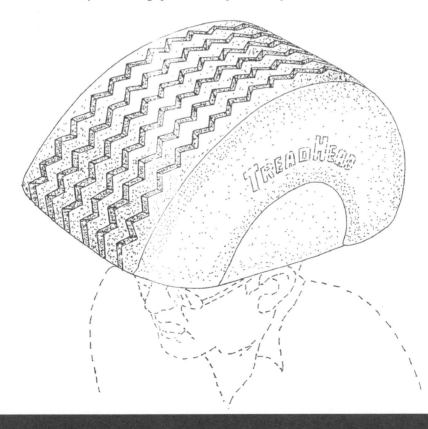

Hat

patent #: US D517782

Isn't that so thoughtful of you, to allow miniature bears to play basketball on your hat. What a good friend you are to shrunken animals.

Neck Wrap/Brace for Holding Items and Belt Article Holder for Same

patent #: US 6929164

We live in an age where organisation is valued over intelligence. Accessories define the organised man. And if you are overwhelmed by your organisational accessories, then there are other accessories designed to help you organise those organisational accessories. Ad infinitum.

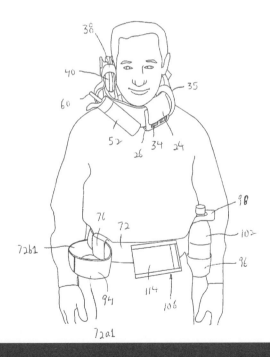

Urban Yoke

patent #: US D508323

For the urban shopper on the go… Now, which bag did I put my eyeballs in?

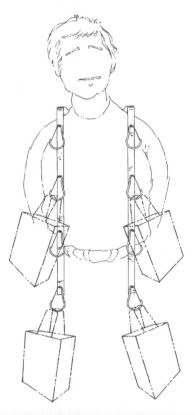

Vibrating, Body-Piercing Jewelry

patent #: US 6865907

I imagine some vibrating piercings are pleasurable, but who benefits from a vibrating nose ring?

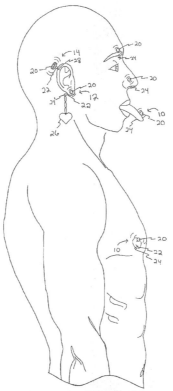

Decorative Valved Tracheostomy Device

patent #: US 6789542

This is probably the only piece of bling that P. Diddy doesn't have. Who says you can't have a hole punched in your throat and still look cool?

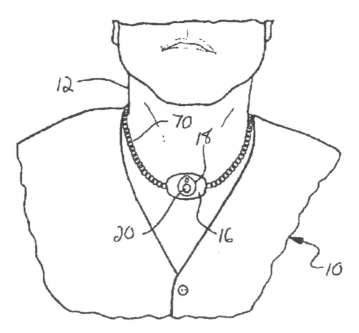

Collar

patent #: US D504984

It is said that, over time, dogs begin to resemble their owners – a process that can be accelerated through coordinated collaring.

In an age when two of the most tricked-out rappers are named Snoop Dogg and Bow Wow, canine bling should be no surprise. What's impressive here is the patent holder's bold suggestion that their design can be enjoyed by both beauty and beast alike. You can wear it while dining at five-star restaurants or even just put it on for a casual afternoon in the back yard, snacking on old turds.

So don't just buy one, buy two. Don't be selfish!

Balance Watch
patent #: US 6840665

Do you walk around with a slightly off-kilter feeling, like one leg is shorter than the other, or like you had a little too much tequila last night? It's an off-balance feeling that's so slight most people wouldn't notice it.

The problem might be your watch. You could be throwing your equilibrium out of whack by wearing just one. So, why not spread time across both wrists? Have "one measuring hours, the other measuring minutes and/or seconds". You'll also be getting that all important, equally-distributed neck movement.

The Balance Watch – keeping time for Obsessive-Compulsives since 2005.

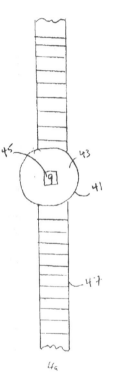

Toothpick Jewelry

patent #: US D527298

Is that spinach between your teeth or caret?
    Display your good hygiene and obscene wealth with this diamond studded toothpick. Will we ever run out of things to bling?

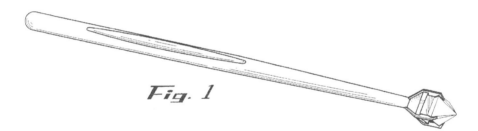

Fig. 1

Footwear

patent #: US D524036

I've heard of women wearing small shoes, but this isn't quite what I had in mind.

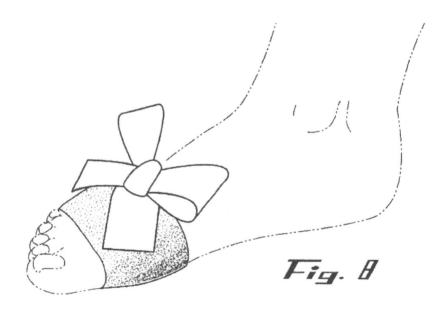

Fig. 8

Bottle Cap Necktie

patent #: US D509944

How was my weekend? Let's just say I got totally hammered and had some creative breakthroughs…

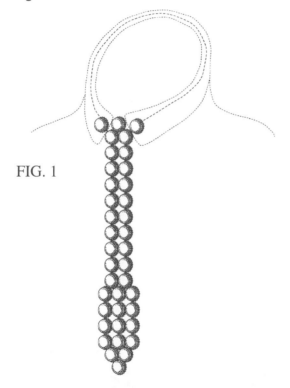

FIG. 1

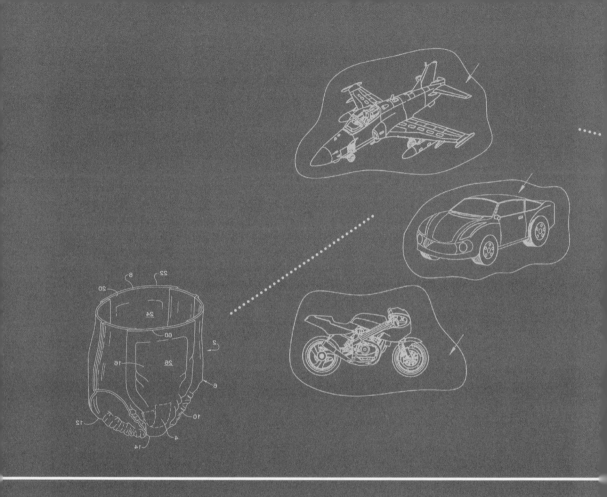

Children

Fetal Educator Strap

patent #: US 6840775

Clean the chalkboards, empty the classes
No more schooling for the masses.
All you really need to know
You'll pick up in utero.

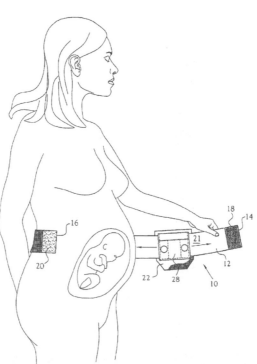

Infant-Operable Remote Controlled Entertainment and Education Device and System

patent #: US 6746299

Alright, enough is enough. Stop it! What exactly are the entertainment needs of an infant? A milky nipple and a zrrbrrt on the tummy not doing the trick anymore? Of course, these traditional entertainments require a human being to be present, and who has time these days to spare love and attention?

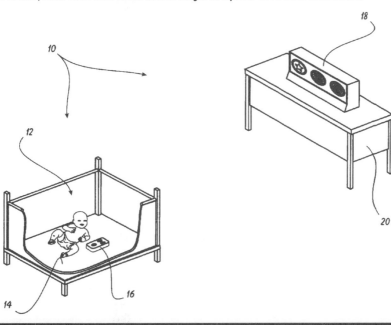

Baby Bottle Accessory

patent #: US 6827317

One day Baby and Panda will be separated. It's a fact of life; as children get older, parents throw away old toys.

But how can Baby live without Panda? Panda, who nursed Baby from her giant, protruding, plastic appendage. Panda, who doubled as Baby's chew toy as poor Baby's teeth began to grow. Panda, who always shouted to the world her religious faith, "God Loves Me" (see illustration).

Yes, one day Panda will be thrown away. For the love of God, no!

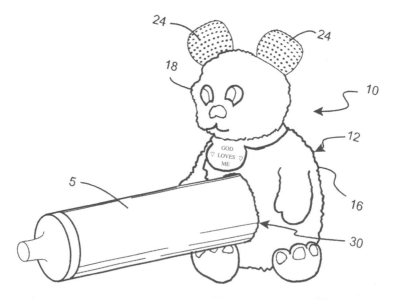

Infant Feeding and Entertainment Support

patent #: US 7048160

This invention is a promising substitute for mothers unable to breastfeed and for hippie fathers wishing to break gender stereotypes (this second conclusion based on the long hair and square jaw of the person in Figure 1).

But this device goes a step further and addresses another, apparently unresolved, problem – how can we make breasts more entertaining?

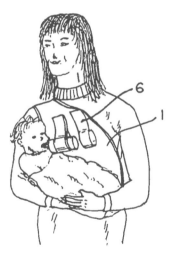

FIG. 1

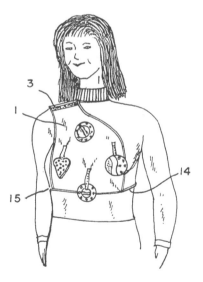

FIG. 3

Thong Diaper

patent #: US D539422

In the paraphrased (and slightly altered) words of Sisqo, "All the scandalous babies in the house show your thong th-thong thong thong." What possible justification is there for a thong nappy? Unfortunately for us, in a design patent you don't need to provide one.

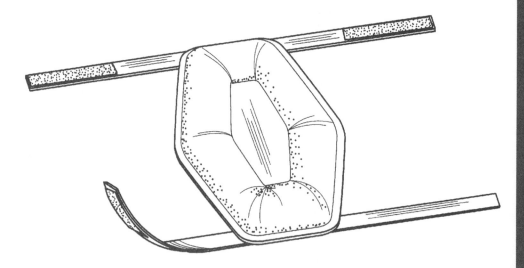

Process for Manufacturing a Toilet Training Article Containing Effervescent Agent

patent #: US 6929819

Incontinence king Kimberly-Clark has added effervescent technology to nappies. Whenever a little kid wees in their shorts, they will experience a "popping", "crackling", "bubbling" or "fizzing" in their nether regions. Supposedly, this will help them on their quest for bowel control. It may also spark nostalgia years later when they experience similar sensations from venereal disease.

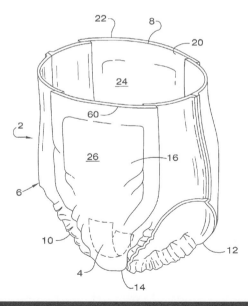

Toilet Training Assembly

patent #: US 6829788

Positive reinforcement is a proven technique of child-rearing: good behaviour should be rewarded.

This inventor combines age-appropriate incentives with technology to help parents with the difficult task of toilet training.

The "assembly" has a built-in motion detector to determine when your little one has "done the deed". Once the loaf has been pinched, the toilet "emits congratulatory sounds", "lights up" and dispenses "a predetermined amount of candy". Bravo! Well done! Come back tomorrow for an encore!

...Wait a minute, it dispenses candy? Aren't we missing an important step here? Hand washing? Especially before sticking something in your mouth?

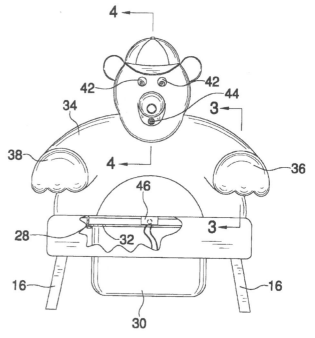

Method for Biodegradable Material Having Water and Uric Acid Activated Color Images

patent #: US 6811403

Do you remember the invisible ink experiment you did in Science? You write a note using lemon juice for ink that can only be read by holding it up to a flame?

This invention is similar, though messier. It's a piece of chemically-treated biodegradable material that contains an invisible image. Drop it in water and an outline forms. Urinate on it and vibrant colours complete the picture!

While it may help you toilet-train your toddler, this is one artwork you won't want to hang on the refrigerator.

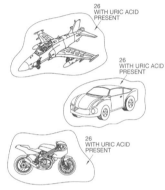

26
WITH URIC ACID PRESENT

26
WITH URIC ACID PRESENT

26
WITH URIC ACID PRESENT

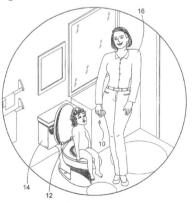

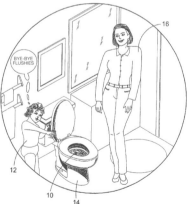

Stroller with CD Player

patent #: US 7077405

"Yo, bitch, plug my iPod in this muthafucka and give me a push!" How much is too much stimulation?

Wagon Cup Holder

patent #: US 6871863

What every sophisticated, trend-setting, latte drinking, wagon pulling tyke needs… along with a twelve-hour shift in a sweatshop and one night in Bangkok with Garry Glitter.

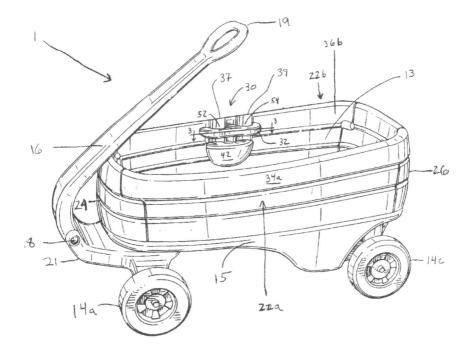

Child Car Seat

patent #: US D533363

"Hey, kid, come here and sit on my lap. Strap yourself in and let me hold your sippie-cup. It's okay, kid, it's the law. You wouldn't want your mother to go to jail now, would you?"

Am I the only one that finds this design a little disturbing?

Scented Doll with the Appearance of an Aged Person

patent #: US 6805607

We all know that old people smell. Finally, there is a doll that acknowledges this reality.

Enough of Barbie and the damaging body-image complexes that she induces in young girls! Enough of GI-Joe and the violent, gun-toting, blind militaristic patriotism he inspires in little boys! Children need a toy that personifies something they can become just by staying alive – a wrinkly, smelly senior citizen.

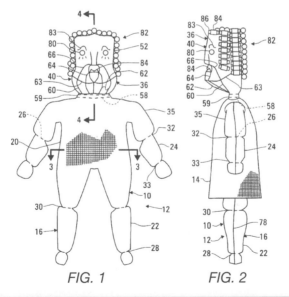

FIG. 1   FIG. 2

Toy Figure Casket Illustrating Dangers of Smoking

patent #: US D494229

My Dolly died the other day,
It really was quite sad.
He was my favourite Dolly,
I was his favourite Dad.

My family gathered round the yard,
We dug a little hole,
Put Dolly in a casket,
Said goodbye to his soul.

It floated up into the sky,
In a stream of smoke.
"Just how Dolly would've wanted"
I said with a tearful choke.

For other dolls could wet themselves
And, when pressed, some could whimper,
But my Dolly was different:
He smoked Lucky Strikes, unfiltered.

Subliminal Recording Device
patent #: US 6940432

What? Is this the bastard love child of Chucky and Teddy Ruxpin? This innocuous-looking teddy bear can be "unnoticeably placed near a child's bed", where it can then impart pre-recorded "affirmations, self-hypnotic suggestions, or subliminal instructions" while the child is in "the subconscious state of sleep". It's perfect for the busy parent who doesn't have the time for traditional brainwashing methods.

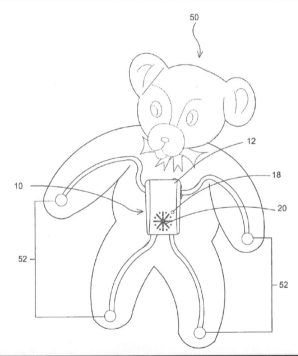

Psychic Seeds Entertaining Growth System

patent #: US 6799762

While a "Psychic Seeds Entertaining Growth System" sounds complicated, it's essentially a flip of a coin that takes six weeks. According to the inventor:

> In its simplest form it allows the user to ask a "question" of the Entertaining Growth System and receive an "answer" by observing the Dynamic Growth of a plant, in this case as a seedling, through labeled holes in a lid.

I love the fact that "Dynamic Growth" is capitalized… as if the concept of plants growing is something new they invented!

So, basically, ask a question, plant a seed, wait six weeks and see which hole the plant emerges from. Presumably the Psychic Seeds also answered "Yes" to the question, "Is this idea good enough to patent?" So, hey, you know it works.

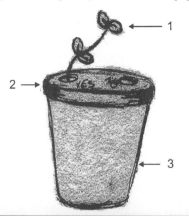

Technique for Diagnosing Attention Deficit Hyperactivity Disorder

patent #: US 6843774

Great patent art. Either it's the way she's desperately gripping the chair, her "daddy double-dosed my Prozac" smile, or the fact that her feet are the size of her torso, something is definitely wrong with this girl.

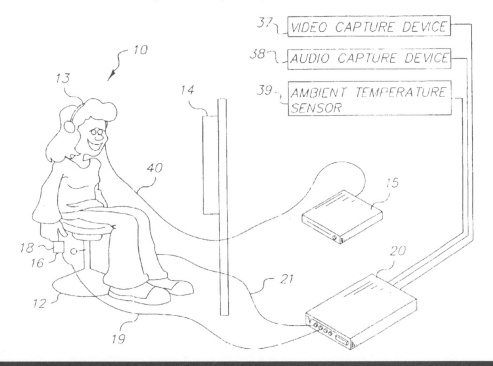

Apparatus for Cat's Cradle Game

patent #: US 7104865

While doing the Cat's Cradle has proved to be a bonding experience for girls over the generations, let's face it… some girls just don't have friends – be they gossips, backstabbers, sluts or just plain new in town… One day it might be you who is down on your luck, with no one willing to convey taut pieces of string from their hands to yours and vice versa.

Or, maybe you do have friends, but they lack the dexterity to accomplish complicated twine transferals, or maybe they simply don't have fingers.

And sometimes isn't it just more rewarding to transpose loops of cord into the rubbery digits of an animatronic companion? There's something reassuring about little girls and robots cooperating in the intimate task of strategically transmitting yarn designs, isn't there?

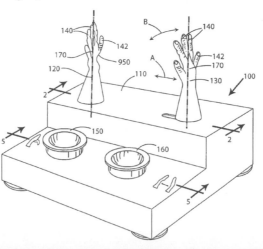

Solo-Operable Seesaw
patent #: US 6872145

If you looked up the word "loner" in the dictionary, you would see someone using this seesaw. Why is an invention like this necessary? The inventors claim that demand is on the rise due to declining birth rates:

> [B]ecause couples are having fewer children today… a sibling… may not always be available to ride the seesaw.

Bullies also pose a problem. Whether they are thrusting the end of the see-saw into the air in an effort to whack passers by in the face, or leaping off at the wrong moment, leaving their co-rider at the mercy of gravity, it seems painful injury is the inevitable outcome.

The see-saw is just too dangerous a weapon to leave in the hands of children.

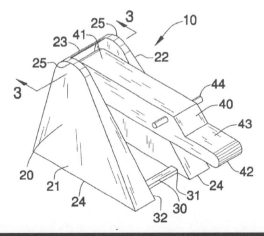

Animals

Edible Animal Greeting Cards and Treats

patent #: US 6838101

While pets have increasingly become a part of the family, who knew they had become sentimental? A pat on the back and a biscuit simply isn't enough.

The inventor anticipates many flavours of card suitable for dogs, cats, horses, birds, rabbits, guinea pigs, and even hamsters and gerbils! I would assume the message would change too? Let's see, I need one "Happy Birthday", one "Good Luck at the Kennel" and a "Sorry, I Cut Your Nuts Off".

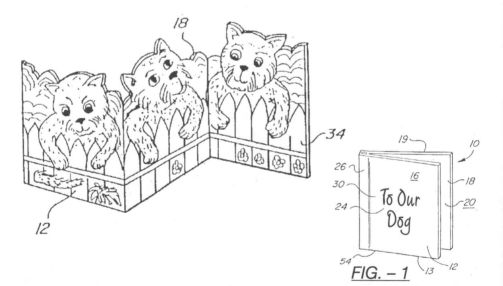

FIG. — 1

Pet Umbrella and Combined Pet Leash and Umbrella

patent #: US 6871616

Imagine you're caught in a thunderstorm, soaked to the bone, as this pampered dachshund swaggers out of the doggy spa and steps into a chauffeured limousine, all the while with an umbrella over its head.

Sometimes justice, like this umbrella, is upside-down.

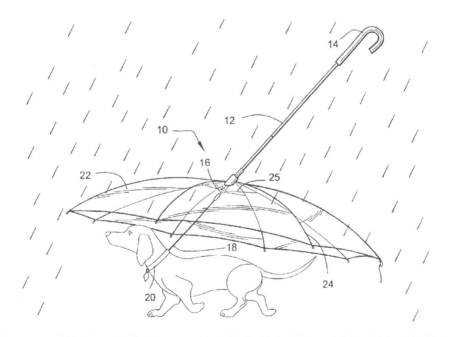

Method of Exercising a Cat

patent #: US 5443036

This "method" patent is one of the more controversial patents issued in recent years. The peculiarity of method patents is that they are not on things, but on ways of doing things. Critics consider the real harm to be from processes such as software algorithms and financial instruments, but US #5443036 threw a cat into the equation, which was just too cute for society to ignore.

The "invention" is a means to motivate a cat's hunting instinct by using a laser pointer. Anyone who's ever tried it will attest to the method's efficacy. If you haven't tried it, do. It's quite hilarious. But just keep in mind that every time you do, you might owe the "inventors" (yes, it took two!) a royalty.

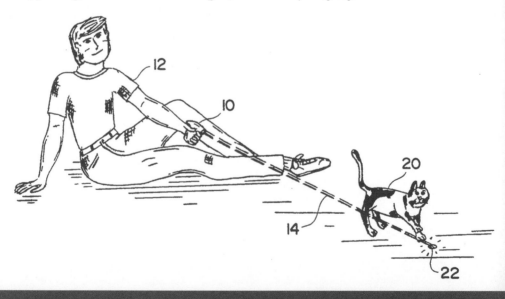

Pet Entertainment Device
patent #: US 7066780

The "Pet Entertainment Device" takes the "Method of Exercising a Cat" to the next level. The advantages I see in this one are that it:

A. attaches the laser directly to the pet, thus not requiring a human;
B. always points in the pet's line of vision, maintaining a constant state of interest (if not insanity); and
C. is no longer cat-specific, spreading the joy to the rest of the domesticated animal kingdom.

Sometimes chasing one's tail gets old.

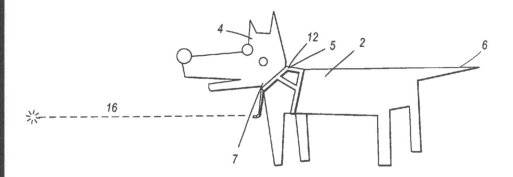

Vending System for Pet Items and Method

patent #: US 6886715

Has there ever been a machine more detrimental to animal-human relationships? If your dog no longer relies upon you as the "treat-master", you may find yourself cut off like a pair of testes at a neutering clinic.

This "vending system" packs "a ball, a container of water or drinking liquid, a pet-food item, a pet grooming item, a pet health item, a non-ball pet toy, a collar, a leash, an I.D. tag, a whistle and a waste disposal kit." All he needs is some pocket money and an opposable thumb, and Rover's going solo.

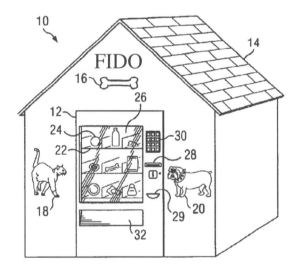

Doggie Poop Freeze Wand

patent #: US 6883462

Behold, the magic poop wand! The problem (as defined in the patent):

1. The clean-up of animal faeces is tedious, smelly, and messy.
2. The disposal of animal faeces causes bulk, odours in trash or disposal areas, and unsanitary conditions.
3. The content of faeces causes distruction [sic] and degradation of properties.
4. The natural body function of our animals is sometimes a nuisance to society.

The solution: kill the furry bastards..!
I mean, use this wand containing a
compressed freezing agent. You
merely press a button and, *voilá*,
an instant poopsicle.

Attachment for Blade of Hockey Stick
patent #: US 6926629

Minnesota resident Martin Dehen has come up with a new use for the hockey stick – cleaning up rubbish from the garden. As the inventor notes, it's great for the nasty stuff, especially "rotten hornet-infested crab apples and dog waste".

Why a hockey stick? Well, here is another option the inventor considered:

> If the waste is to be flung by hand to a desired location, such as a compost heap, the waste may crumble upon the head of one who throws the waste.

As I believe the great Thomas Edison once said, "There's nothing that inspires my inventive spirit quite like a scalp full of crumbling dog shit."

Dehen goes to the root of the problem: why fling dried dog shit with one's hand when those kindly Canadians have given us a stick that can hit an object "with great force, with great control, and over a relatively great distance"? And so, the Turd Burglar™ was born.

Fig.-2

Flush Toilet for a Dog

patent #: US 6769382

This doggy toilet (demonstrated here by this rare dog/cow/goat hybrid) permits your pet to answer nature's call in the safety of your own home.

But this canine crapper is not only a win for dogs and their owners; it's also a boon for the poor. As philanthropist/inventor Chui-Wen Chiu declares:

> Wisdom is bred by education and wisdom brings further wisdom, for this reason, I would donate 30% of the profit derived from this invention for the education of gifted students from poor families.

Education begets wisdom begets doggy toilets begets education. It's shocking this correlation hadn't been discovered earlier. The world gets better one flush at a time.

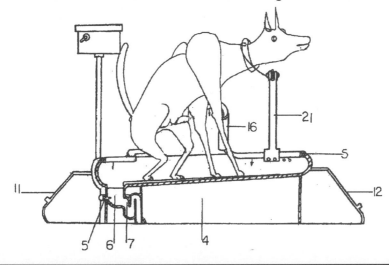

Apparatus for Determining Dog's Emotions by Vocal Analysis of Barking Sounds and Method for the Same

patent #: US 6761131

From the patent:

> The present invention relates to an apparatus of determining animals' emotions from vocal analysis of barking sounds, and more particularly, it relates to an apparatus of determining dogs' emotions by vocally analyzing barking sounds.

Sit. Stay. Bark slowly and clearly. Do *not* urinate on the mic stand.

This device is apparently for emotionally retarded pet owners and those yearning to become a dog whisperer. The invention claims to pick up on such hard-to-detect feelings of "loneliness", "frustration", "aggressiveness", "assertiveness", "happiness" and, most oddly, "wistfulness".

Aww… is the little doggy feeling pensive?

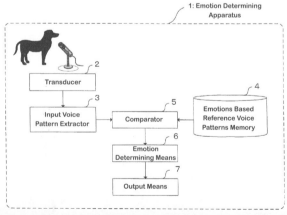

1: Emotion Determining Apparatus

2 Transducer

3 Input Voice Pattern Extractor

5 Comparator

4 Emotions Based Reference Voice Patterns Memory

6 Emotion Determining Means

7 Output Means

Bird Perch

patent #: US 6860237

You know how it is with birds. Give them some seed, they want a cracker. Give them a cracker, they want to be your best friend.

    According to the inventor, using this perch is safer than allowing the bird to sit on your shoulder, where they can "peck, scratch, or bite the person's face, ears, head, etc.". As you can see, the guy's shirt is pretty ripped up and it appears as if his right eye has been pecked out! The way this parrot's head is cocked, it looks like Polly's got some major attitude. She tore this cracker up!

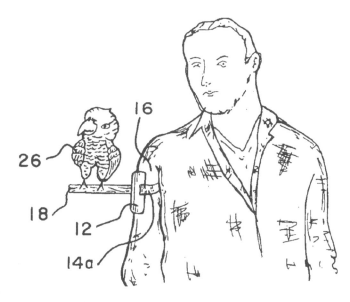

Animal Garment

patent #: US 6820574

If you really want to spoil your dog, take Rover to the day spa. In between the whirlpool tubs and the therapeutic massage (Shiatsu or Shi Tzu?), pamper him with a little Chinese medicine…

   This isn't any ordinary dog-sweater; it's specially designed to contact "various acupressure points… to reduce anxiety behaviour in the wearer." This must be the most comfortable garment ever – and it's for a bloody dog!

   (Question for the inventor: does a neutered animal still have a "Conception Vessel acupressure meridian"?)

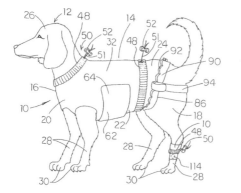

FIG.1

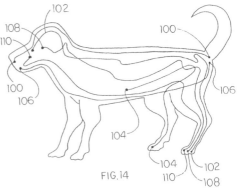

FIG.14

Portable Electrical Mouse Trap

patent #: US 6865843

Ralph Waldo Emerson is attributed as saying, "Build a better mousetrap, and the world will beat a path to your door." Each year, new inventors attempt to outdo their predecessors, and each year, mousetraps become a little more bizarre.

To its credit, this mousetrap is more humane than most. It's not like it's trying to hide. It's shaped like a cat! It practically broadcasts to the mouse community, "Hey, look at me, I'm your mortal enemy, you might want to stay away!"

How then, does it work? This cat-shaped, electrical terminator tempts its prey with a "cheese fragrance" that wafts from deep within its abdomen. The passing rodent must then choose between two powerful instincts: a sensible fear of sharp-fanged housecats and an unquenchable addiction to smelly cheese.

Basically, it kills the idiots and the junkies.

In the accompanying patent illustrations, the mouse falls for the bait. Against better judgment, it crawls right into the gaping jaws of its feline foe. Once in the cat's abdomen, the jaws shut and a vacuum sucks the mouse into the collection chamber, where the mouse is then promptly suffocated. And then, to signify that the chamber is full, the cat's eyes emit a menacing, post-digestion glow.

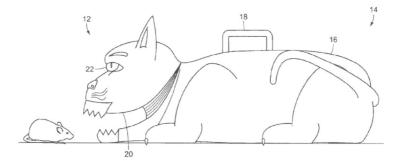

Rodent Catching Apparatus

patent #: US 6739086

As described in the patent:

> When a rodent enters upon the metal ramp and comes within about ¼ inch of
> the baited electrode, it is electrocuted and falls to the bottom of the bucket,
> which contains a pool of water.

Tempt them, shock them and drown them. Unique, cruel and unusual!

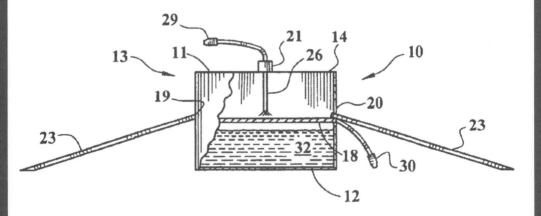

Method and System for Measuring Mobility of a Tested Animal

patent #: US 6799535

First, notice the little mouse floating in the tank of water. Good. Now, read the following statement of purpose from the patent:

> A measurement result from the forced swimming test for a tested animal, such as a mouse, is usually used as reference for evaluating whether the tested animal has symptoms of depression.

I object to the term "forced swim test". Can't we condense that to one word... I don't know... "drowning"? Apparently, the happier mice will fight for their lives, wheras the gloomy, dejected ones won't try that hard. Aren't there less cruel ways to test for depression? I can't see it catching on in human diagnosis...

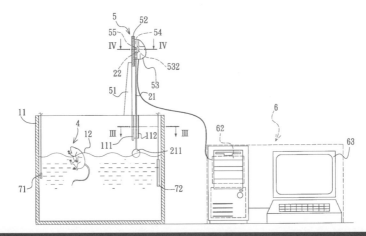

Robotic Device for Locomotor Training
patent #: US 6880487

Amidst all the Christopher Reeve brouhaha there was another story that went unreported, one of an American hero battling impossible odds. While the nation mourned for the loss of Superman, another famously strong crime fighter suffered a near fatal injury of his own. After a close nuzzle with death, a beloved mouse was fighting his own battle with paraplegia.

But his indomitable spirit shone through. With hope, determination and assistance from this "Robotic Device for Locomotor Training", we may one day again hear his Mighty cry, "Here I come to save the day!"

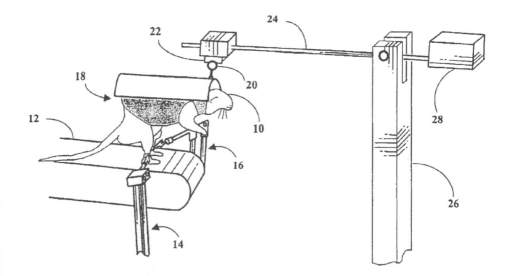

Animal Restraining Apparatus and Animal Experiment for Using the Same

patent #: US 6789510

"Grabbing the rat by its tail" has finally got a patent. Now you can cut a hole in its brain and monitor it "for more than 72 hours"! Never has cruelty been so cute.

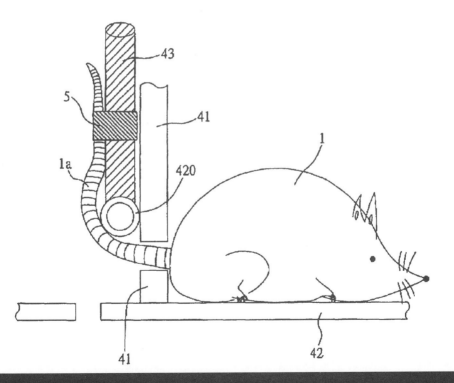

Immobilization Device
patent #: US 6901884

From the patent:

> The invention provides a device for use in partially or fully immobilizing animals such as cattle, sheep and the like. The device includes a probe for insertion in the anal canal of the animal, the probe comprising a pair of spaced electrodes connected by way of electrical conductors to a power source. The power source provides a pulsed electrical current.

While I can come to terms with using animals for food and research, this arse-shocker is a step too far!

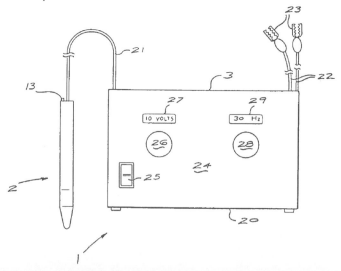

Animal Sorting and Grading System Using MRI to Predict Maximum Value

patent #: US 6877460

Wait a minute… Cows get free MRIs and there are 40 million Americans without health insurance?

While we humans regard MRIs as life-saving instruments, for cows they may be harbingers of death. A doctor might do an MRI and say, "Sorry, it looks like you only have six months to live", while a rancher might say, "Sorry, it looks like you only have six months to live… until you're absolutely delicious!"

This invention seeks to use MRIs to determine "the number of days on feed needed to reach maximum carcass value." Don't worry, my bovine friend, like James Dean and Marilyn Monroe, you'll be going out at the top of your game!

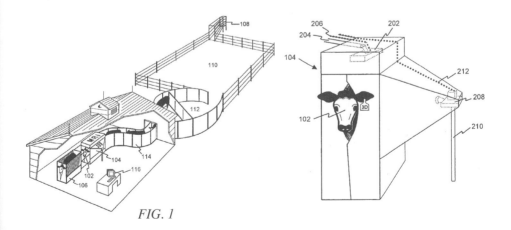

FIG. 1

Animal Keeping Device and a Method for Animal Keeping

patent #: US 7051680

Does a treadmill make them free range?
    This little beauty from Sweden promotes healthy exercise and energy conservation. The floor of the pen is a conveyer belt. As the cow walks, the belt carries in food and fresh straw and dumps out cow pies and other waste. Ingenious! Multiple pens can allow a whole herd to move at once. Yee-haw! It's like an old-fashioned cattle drive, only stationary.

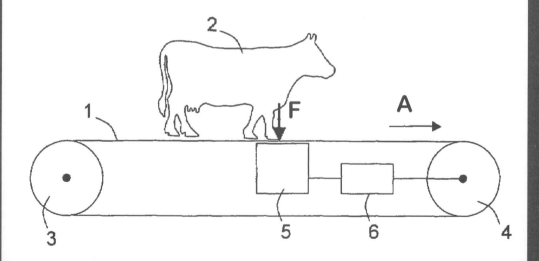

Spinal Cord Removal Tool with Adjustable Blades

patent #: US 6805696

Ouch. The words "spinal cord grinders" make me cringe. This device from the meat-packing industry certainly has to be one of the creepiest inventions I've ever seen. It makes me want to be either a vegetarian or a horror film director.

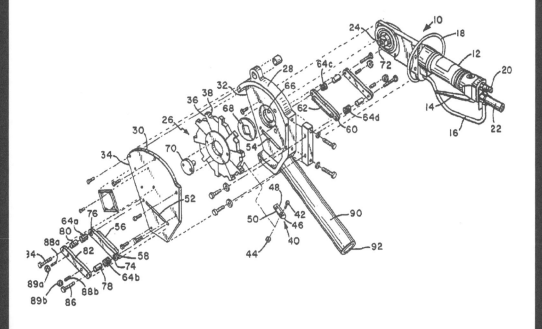

Method and Apparatus for Head Removal

patent #: US 6776701

And I thought the science of head-removal died with Mr. Guillotine! This contraption is used in the pork industry to make sure we get as much meat as possible from those chubby little hog-necks.

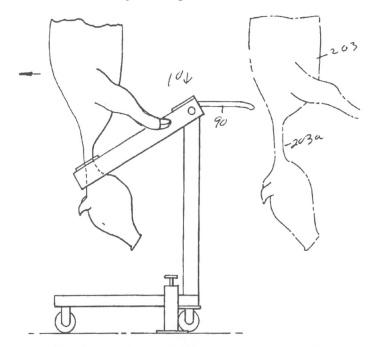

Intravaginal Retention Device for a Tailed Animal

patent #: US 6739285

When a cow wags her tail, it's because she's happy. That or she's trying to remove the large dildo that's been stuck in her vagina for the last two weeks.

This "Intravaginal Retention Device", assigned to agriculture giant Monsanto, is inserted into a cow's vagina to monitor their oestrus cycle so ranchers know when the cow is ready for inseminating. In the dairy industry, for every cow that isn't pregnant, "there is an economic loss of between $1.00-$3.00 per day".

(Wait a minute – a cow makes more in a day than half the world's population, just for having her tits squeezed? Where's Dr. Moreau when you need him?)

Unfortunately for the cow, this invention makes it harder to remove the device by attaching it to her tail. Sorry Bessie, back to being bare-hooved and pregnant.

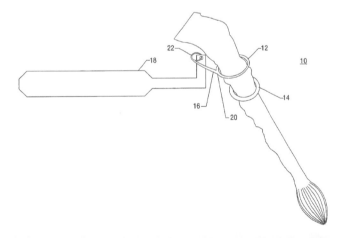

System for Removing Dead Animals
patent #: US 7097025

Judging by the artistry of the patent illustration, this contraption was most likely invented by a twelve-year-old in need of psychological counselling.

In the drawing our bald, belted and pant-booted farm worker has the unpleasant task of protecting our food supply by removing the dead chickens (as indicated with Xs for eyes) from the peep (yes, that's what a group of chickens is called!).

While the farmer may be unhappy (emotional state deduced from the slightly down-turned mouth), how lucky we are to have him hanging, bucketing and removing these deceased fowl. But a full seven out of thirteen of the chickens in this coop appear to have died! Perhaps there is a larger problem at this facility?

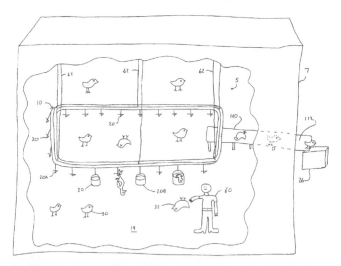

Process for the Utilization of Ruminant Animal Methane Emissions

patent #: US 6982161

Global warming is no joke, and neither is this specially-designed garment for trapping cow belches.

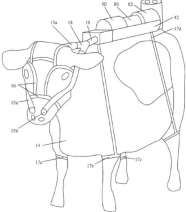

Cow belches contain methane, a notorious greenhouse gas that is twenty times more effective at trapping heat in the atmosphere than carbon dioxide. This bovine backpack traps the nasty flatulence and then pumps it into a special capsule where micro-organisms consume the carbon-rich gas.

As if saving the atmosphere weren't enough of an accomplishment, the inventor claims that after their brief, micro-fabulous lives are over, these organisms can be harvested as useful biomass. According to the patent, "Such biomass can be processed and sold as a nutritional foodstuff[!]" Mmm… foodstuff…

Ingestible Chewing Gum for Animals

patent #: US 6803061

If the above invention fails to deliver its promise, we can at least take some comfort in the knowledge that we'll all swelter to our early deaths in a sweet-smelling environment.

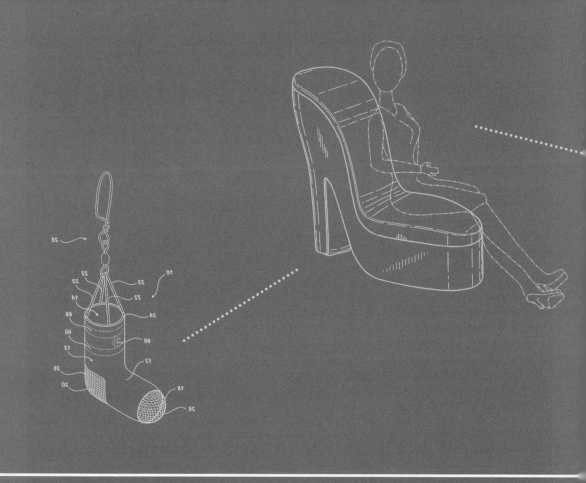

Work
and Home

Office Gym Exercise Kit

patent #: US 7137935

The cubicle has become more than just a semi-private workspace. In today's workaholic culture it also doubles as a dining room, art gallery and YouTube mini-theatre. So why not use it as a gym?

   This kit provides a full range of arm, leg and back exercises. All you need is a chair, a desire to get fit and a willingness to look stupid.

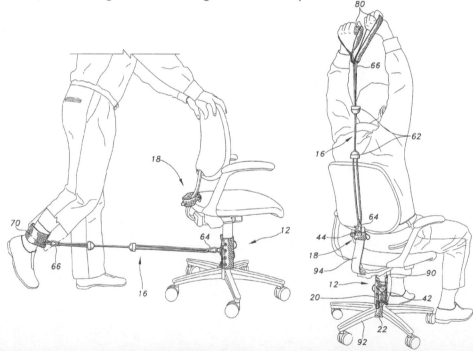

Work Space Divider

patent #: US D530104

If your work environment is as chilly as the Arctic (whether that's in terms of temperature, emotion or both), you might want to take a lesson from the Eskimo and ask your office manager for a Cubigloo (made up name, not yet trademarked!). What better way to alienate yourself from the rest of the workforce?

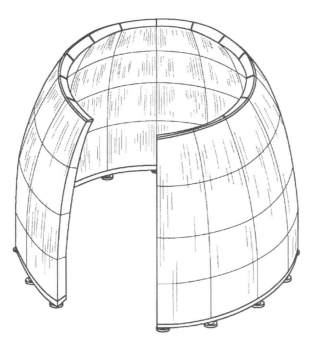

Retractable Table Top for a Toilet
patent #: US 6983493

Some of the best ideas come when you're sitting on the loo. So why not take your work to the bog?

Rafik Shaumyan has at last conquered the "shortcomings" of standard facilities. He has thoroughly analyzed society's plebian use of the crapper and restored its royal dignity. As he puts it:

> The toilet seat can more rightly be called "the throne" if certain conditions are met above and beyond the simple support and flush provisions.

Amen. Rafik plans to supply toilet paper (thank goodness), cigarettes, matches, reading material and even paper to write a shopping list on… Conveniences fit for a king.

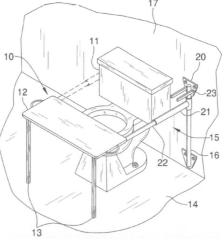

Convertible Seat with Contoured-Front for Localized Body Heat Dispersion and Pressure Reduction

patent #: US 6997516

We sit too much. In school rooms and offices, our collective ass is grass – planted and growing. Over the past twenty years, ergonomics specialists have come up with various ways of improving our posture. But in all this time, what has been done *for the balls?*

Between my time-consuming obsession with the U.S. Patent Office and my overheated, sandwiched testicles, I may never reproduce. But at least there's hope, thanks to what I dub "The Ball Chair".

With the addition of a simple, recessed centre, inventor Jianqing Lan's invention lets your scrotum stretch all the way to the shag carpet "so that the dispersion of body heat from that area via air circulation will not be blocked by the seat base, and… the pressure between the testes area and the seat base will be reduced or eliminated, thereby improving the physiological condition for sperm…"

So make the switch. Email your boss and let him or her know that your testes need to breathe!

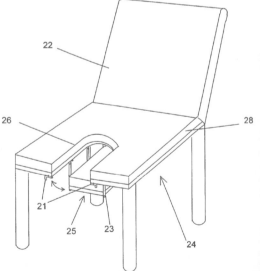

Amusement Device That Senses Odorous Gases in a Bathroom

patent #: US 6966840

With some patents, it's best to just let the inventor do the talking. Webb T. Nelson of Woodinville, WA, what have you blessed us with?

> A novelty device that makes humorous statements when a person is having a bowel movement in a confined bathroom. The device includes an automated character, such as a bird in a birdcage, a skunk with a gasmask or some other character. Within the device is a gas sensor for detecting at least one gas emitted during a bowel movement… Once activated, a humorous audible message is broadcast. The message may say "What a stench! Somebody open the window! There are rules against cruelty to animals!" A countless number of messages can be used… There is a fine line between a novelty device that is funny and a novelty device that is annoying.

A fine line, which might have been crossed…

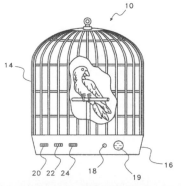

Aromatic Travel Mask

patent #: US 6758215

Frequent fliers may appreciate this all-in-one sensory deprivation mask, which can filter out unwanted sounds, light and smells. Perhaps most valuable is its ability to filter out dangerous microbes, pollens, and allergens from the re-circulated air of the "modern travel environment".

Yet, deep beneath the patent's utility lurks an unexpected cry of marketing desperation:

> The mask is preferably provided with markings which may be in the form of amusing characters, advertising or slogans and the like to encourage use of the aromatic travel mask.

If adults start wearing little bunny masks in airplanes I think it's time we update the USA P.A.T.R.I.O.T. Act with a "Kill da Wabbit" clause.

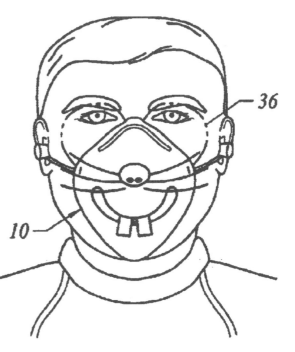

Business Card with Integrated Paper Cell Phone

patent #: US 7058365

In an age of disposable technology, this business card/cell phone combo fits right in. Conductive ink is used to print the circuit directly on the card, and the microphones and speakers are constructed from the paper. I can't attest to the feasibility of the technology, but given the patent is assigned to the Hewlett-Packard Development Company, the invention may have a future.

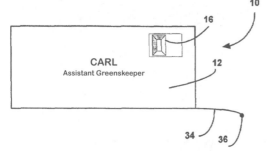

As the patent illustration demonstrates, these cards are not just for wealthy Silicon Valley dot-com trendsetters, but also for one-monikered, subordinate hedge-trimmers like "Carl, Assistant Greenskeeper". Ace.

Business Card Made from Edible Material

patent #: US D493601

Because that's exactly what you want to do with a business card. Eat it.

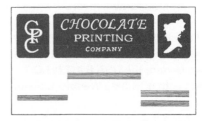

Safety Cone for Warning of Slippery Conditions

patent #: US D514464

Banana = Slippery. Now that's effective design!

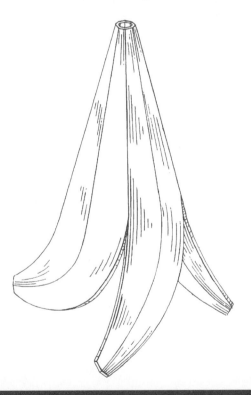

Light Bulb Changer

patent #: US 6826983

How many inventors does it take to change a light bulb? One, but first he needs to get patent protection.

While light bulbs themselves are becoming more and more efficient, light bulb changing, on the other hand, seems to be going in the opposite direction.

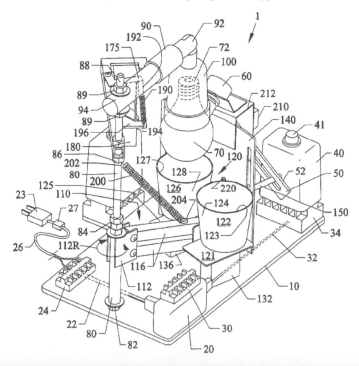

Yoke

patent #: US D503023

Why would one bother getting a patent on a yoke design? Is there a hot market for bucket-hauling devices right now? And is someone without indoor plumbing who might actually need a yoke really going to give a rat's ass about your "intellectual property"?

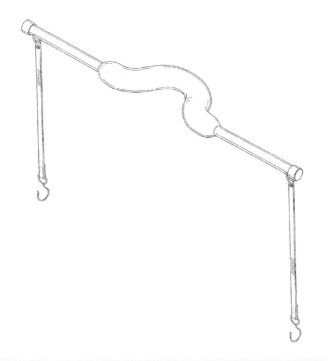

Picture Frame Figurine

patent #: US D528805

This picture frame is the only way to commemorate achieving the most difficult of yoga poses – the head-up-your-asana. Horrific.

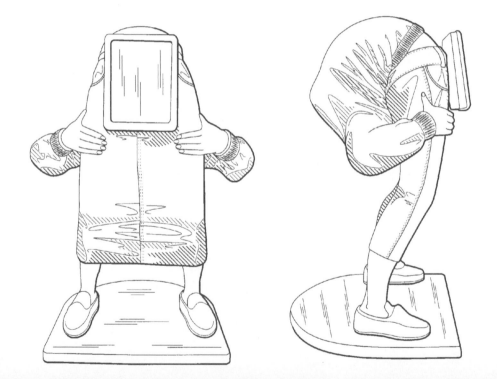

North Wildwood Flyin' Socks

patent #: US 7043976

There's something appealing about the North Wildwood Flyin' Sock. Not in the typical "oh-my-god-someone-tied-a-rope-to-a-sock-and-patented-it" kind of way. It has a certain whimsy. It's nice and simple. It's just an open-toed sock that blows nicely in the breeze, in a somewhat better way than previous sock contraptions.

And it hails from America's often tacky, yet unpretentious South Jersey shore. It's not some uptight, proper "Greenwich, Connecticut Flying Sock". It's a laid back, good-time loving "North Wildwood Flyin' Sock", indicating wind direction not because it has to, but because, well, why the hell not?

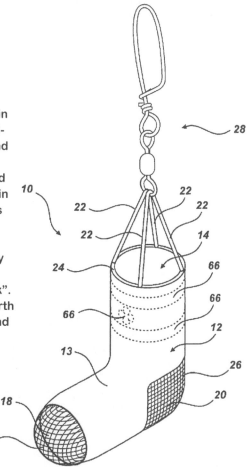

Automatic Bed Making Apparatus

patent #: US 7036164

It's heartening to see an inventor work really hard so that the rest of us can be lazy. But at what point is it overkill?

   This invention "includes a vision device that evaluates and detects the current state of the bedding… and a computing device that determines the process of making the bed." A robotic arm then swings out and puts everything back in order. How much crap do we need just to maintain our other crap?

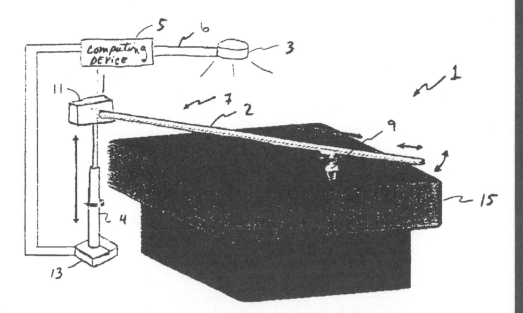

Adaptive Alarm System
patent #: US 6838994

It knows when you are sleeping, it knows when you're awake...

    This alarm clock uses a surveillance camera to determine the depth of your sleep and then adjusts different environmental conditions in the room (turns on lights, turns up music, etc.) to wake you up in a "nonviolent manner".

    Doesn't sound like too much to ask for, does it?

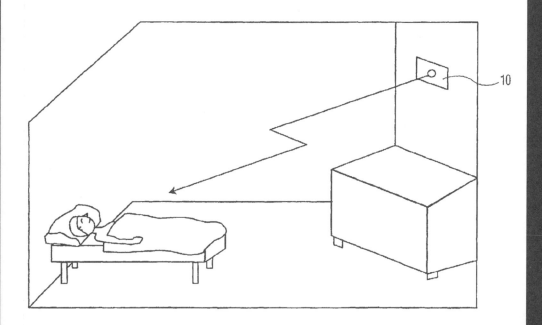

Cajun Dreamcatcher

patent #: US D502755

Because you don't want to let that dream of your home insurance paying for Hurricane Katrina damage get away...

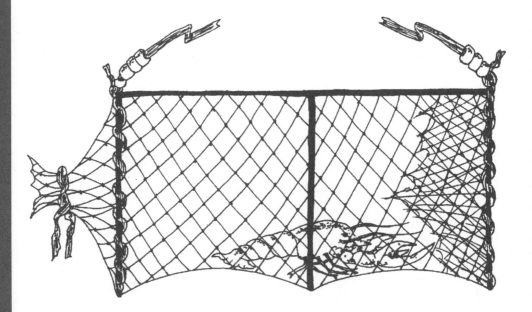

Methods of Promoting Sleep Systems

patent #: US 6997070

Buying the right mattress is an important decision. Mattresses are expensive and you spend a third of your life on one.

Undoubtedly, making the sale is important for the mattress seller, hence this patent on a method "to determine… the proper combination of mattress and pillow…"

I'm not going to bore you with the details, but judging strictly by the patent illustrations, this technique involves having David Hasselhoff perform jiu-jitsu moves on you. Only the Hoff could be such a bad ass. He will grab you by the arm, measure your "resistive force", and send you home with a cushy Posturepedic.

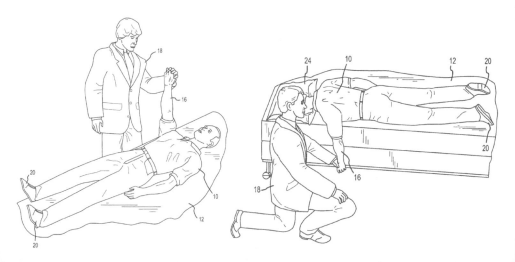

Wave Bed

patent #: US D518972

Water bed technology
gone bad.

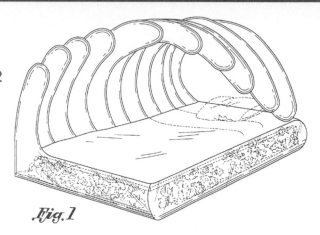

Fig.1

Half-Pipe Bed

patent #: US D517829

Since when is sleeping an X-Game?

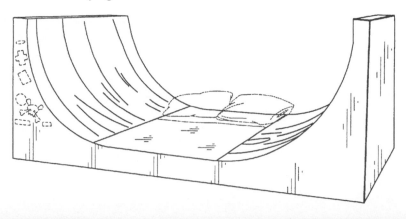

Dividable Mattress

patent #: US 7082634

For when you and your spouse can't kiss and make up...

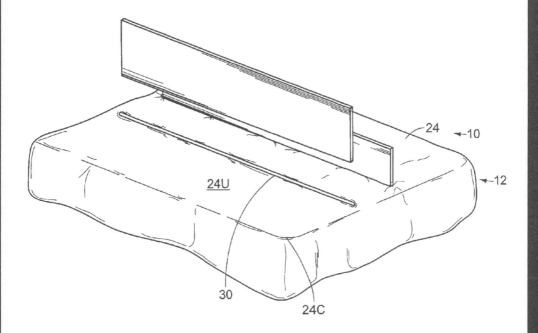

Shoe Chair
patent #: US D519289

At last there's a high-heeled
shoe that is actually comfortable.

Sofa
patent #: US D526506

Um, okay, sure… it's a sofa.
Where exactly do I sit?

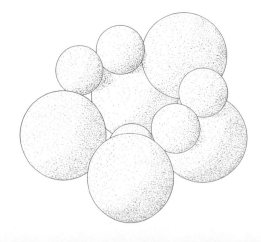

Recliner Handle

patent #: US D502087

Go ahead, take my seat.

Process of Converting a Vehicle into a Utility Structure

patent #: US 6764083

This invention covers a new type of vehicle recycling. Seeing as so many people are content to leave their junked jalopies in their front gardens on breeze blocks, why not use them as "utility structures"?

In a provocative series of illustrations, the inventor shows some glorious transformations of this minivan into a storage room, a greenhouse and a guest house – now that's hospitality!

The inventor also proposes using it as a tornado shelter. Of course, first you have to dig the hole and figure out how to drop the car in there at a not-quite ninety-degree angle. Good luck.

Presumably the inventor was thinking more Birmingham, Alabama, than Birmingham, West Midlands…

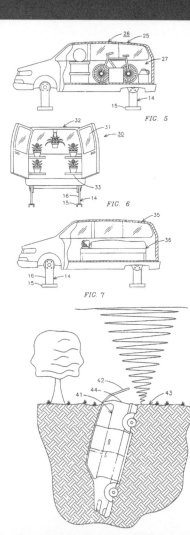

FIG. 5

FIG. 6

FIG. 7

Storm Shelter

patent #: US 6948281

Like any good storm shelter, this one meets all the essential requirements. It is "large enough to hold an entire family, yet still… capable of fitting beneath a mobile home." Judging by the accompanying diagram, the rest of this lady's family are very small indeed.

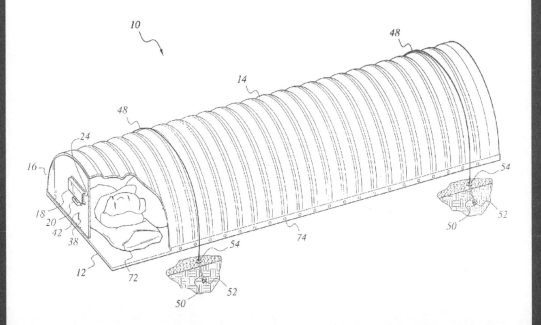

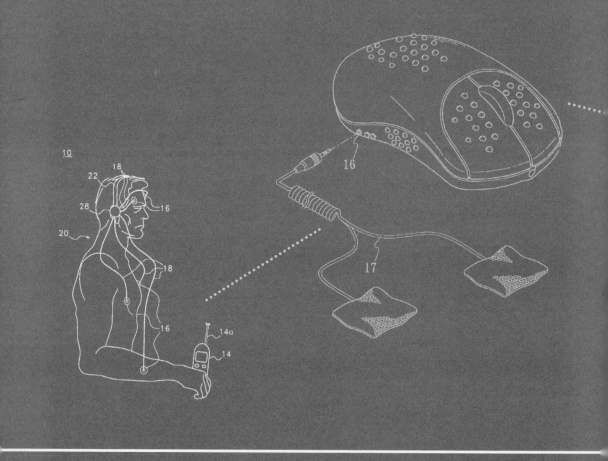

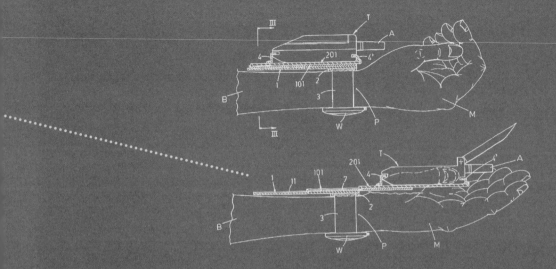

Science and Technology

Device for the Quick and Easy Use of a Small Size Cellular Telephone

patent #: US 6796467

This quick-draw mobile phone bears an uncanny resemblance to Travis Bickle's handgun sling in *Taxi Driver*. Be thankful that you only have to suffer a horrible Robert De Niro impression on the printed page:

"Are you talking to *me*? Are *you* talking to me? Seriously, I have really bad reception right now, and you're breaking up. *Are you talking to me?*"

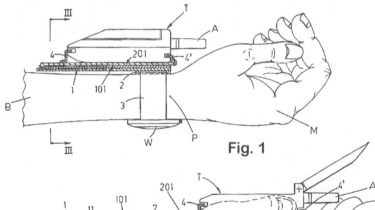

Fig. 1

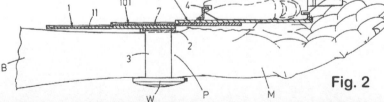

Fig. 2

Electronic Device with Concealed Firearm System

patent #: US 6778811

If talking to your relatives makes you want to shoot yourself in the face, this mobile phone could be the one for you. Hit a sequence of buttons and it fires a bullet out of the antennae. So it's up to you; you can either be a contract killer, or a pay-as-you-talk killer. Just don't shoot your own ear off.

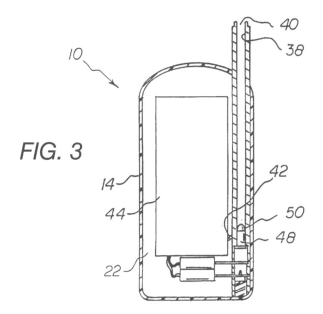

FIG. 3

Sensing Phone Apparatus and Method
patent #: US 7003335

AT&T used to advertise that with their service you could "reach out and touch someone". Of course, they meant it figuratively. This invention, assigned to the InterDigital Technology Corporation, does it literally.

Sensors capture your "physical and/or mental conditions" and then communicate these to the person on the other end via "a series of acupuncture needles" that may be "integrated into a wearable body item such as a glove, body shirt, full body garment, mask or the like." So keep the conversation pleasant!

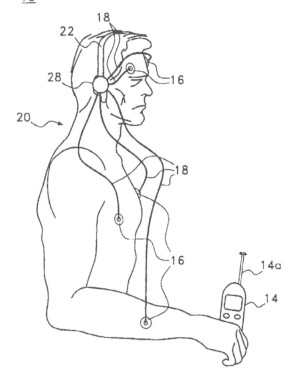

Personal Massaging Apparatus and Method

patent #: US 6978164

While the previous sensory mobile phone patent might have left a little to the imagination, this invention goes straight to the crotch, bringing new meaning to the phrase "booty call".

As suggested by the illustration it can stimulate "nearly every part of the male or female anatomy". The inventor describes an "extended ring" service in which the phone considerately provides "a prolonged period of… sexual stimulation… [so that] the user may achieve climax."

So if you call and she doesn't answer, it's because she really likes you.

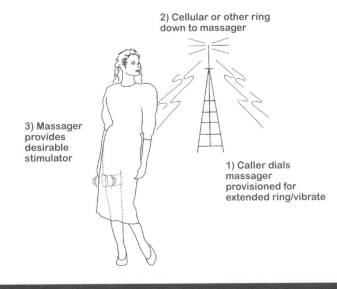

2) Cellular or other ring down to massager

3) Massager provides desirable stimulator

1) Caller dials massager provisioned for extended ring/vibrate

Recording, Transmission and/or Playback of Data Representing an Airflow

patent #: US 6923079

The telefan – what a long awaited invention. Does it transmit the bad breath as well?

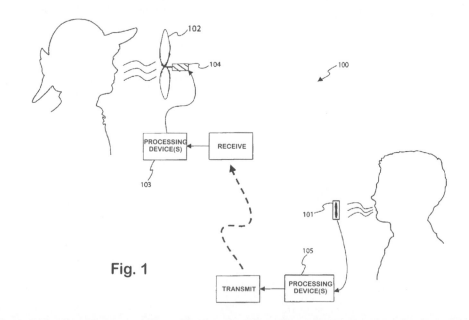

Fig. 1

Voice Communication Concerning a Local Entity

patent #: US 7113911

This has to be just one of the strangest patent illustrations I've ever seen. Is this the future of telephone help lines? "I am a plant. How can I help You?" The patent explains:

> The voice service thus acts as a voice dialog proxy for the plant and gives the impression to the person… that they are conversing with the plant.

And what a stimulating conversation that will be! "How are the seedlings doing? Your leaves are looking lovely – photosynthesis sure has been kind!"

If you've ever wanted "voice interaction with a local dumb device" might I suggest going to your local pub?

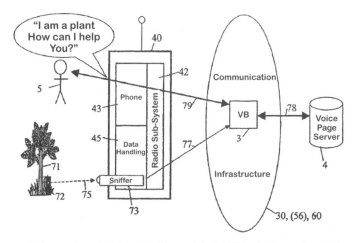

Electronic Device to Detect and Generate Music from Biological Microvariations in a Living Organism

patent #: US 6743164

Apparently plants have a lot to tell us, only we haven't been listening. One use for this invention is to generate "music from electrical variations in a house plant". Not only do plants want to talk to us, but they want to sing to us as well.

According to the inventors, plants "are capable of some sort of rudimentary 'feelings'." The invention detects these "feelings" and outputs the data to a music-making device, giving them the voice they never had. So long, Britney Spears. Hello, Broccoli Spears. Or should that be "Shears"?

Metal-Over-Metal Devices and the Method for Manufacturing Same

patent #: US 6949781

What remnants of Fascism lurk in your computer? The swastika makes an unexpected reappearance in this recently patented microchip capacitor. Hey, a good shape is a good shape. When it comes to processor speeds, there's no time for political correctness.

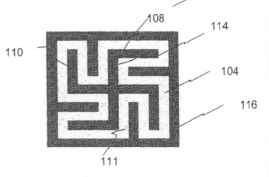

Computer Mouse
for Electronic Therapy

patent #: US 6847846

This mouse purportedly heals its operator by "applying the Chinese ancient principles of acupuncture". It sends "a strong pulse of electric current" though the user's hand. I wonder how the ancient Chinese acupuncture masters would react if knew their wisdom is being dispensed to any fool with a USB port.

They'd probably roll over on their beds of needles.

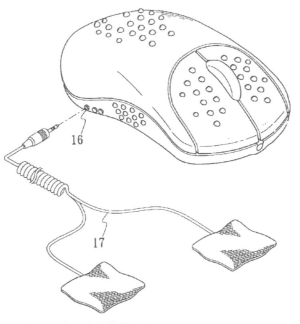

Battery Charger Amusement Device

patent #: US 6995542

Is charging batteries not as exciting as it used to be? Does the thought of all that pent up electrical energy no longer give you pleasurable sensations?

Well, then, silly, it's time to get a "Battery Charger Amusement Device". It's as much fun as toasting bread!

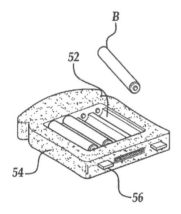

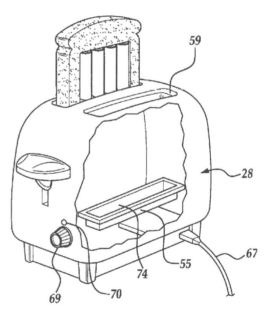

Nuclear Waste Disposal System

patent #: US 6846967

Got some nuclear waste you need to get rid of? Why not dump it in a sub-sea volcano? Is it safe? I'm sure the inventor knows which toxic substances are safe to put in the ocean. After all, he is from New Jersey.

Am I a paranoid freak, or does it seem like a mistake to take a catastrophe waiting to happen and toss it in the middle of a disaster already in progress?

The containers of waste are not actually dropped directly into the cone of the volcano, but off to the side, in the path of the flowing lava. And what if you dump your containers and there's not enough lava to hide the evidence? No problem! According to the inventor, "if the lava flow is deemed inadequate high explosives may be used to increase the lava flow by breaking the volcano walls." Did he just say to drop explosives into a volcano? I'd buy that DVD.

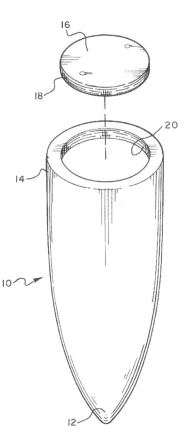

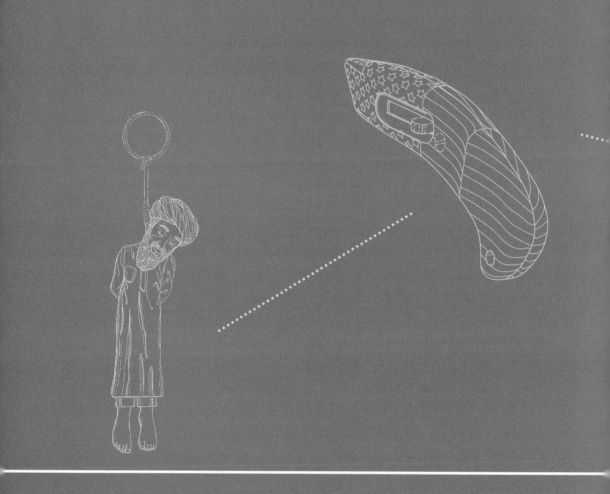

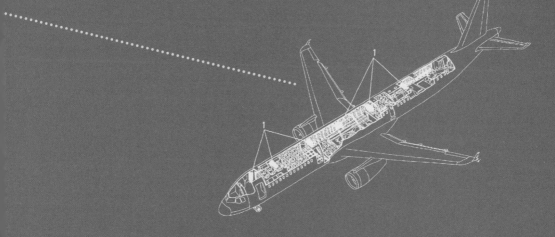

Post 9/11

Aircraft Anti-Terrorism Security System

patent #: US 6844817

Not exactly a silly patent, but too interesting for me to resist. Airbus, the European airplane manufacturer, filed this application for their anti-terror system on September 21, 2001, just ten days after the 9/11 attacks. There have been many patents on anti-terror systems in recent years, but this one carries some extra weight since it is held by a company that could actually implement it.

The main component of the invention is a buffer zone between the main cabin and the cockpit. Any terrorist trying to storm the cockpit would find themselves trapped and assaulted by an array of anti-terror devices such as "a high intensity strobe light", a "high intensity noise generator", "fogging gas", and "knock-out gas". The flight attendant or pilot can also tranquilize the bastard using a remote-controlled night-vision camera equipped with a dart gun.

Once you've incapacitated the terrorist, you can open a trapdoor leading to a confinement cell "strong enough to withstand a firearm discharge and a bomb explosion", and equipped with a nozzle providing additional "knock-out gas".

Enjoy the flight!

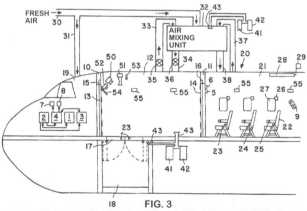

FIG. 3

Aircraft Security System

patent #: US 6877694

Do you have difficulty sleeping on aeroplanes? Bring on the terrorists! Frequent fliers who've forgotten their neck pillows may welcome a few Al-Qaeda members on one of these planes. The security system allows the crew to pump a sweet, gaseous lullaby to the entire cabin. It consists of "a plurality of first switched triggers located in the cockpit, so that a stored paralysing gas [can] be expelled by the expulsion means and inundate the passenger cabin with complete paralysis of all people in said cabin."

Spared a messy death at the hands of Al-Qaeda, but temporarily paralysed by a perma-tanned trolley-dolly. Sweet.

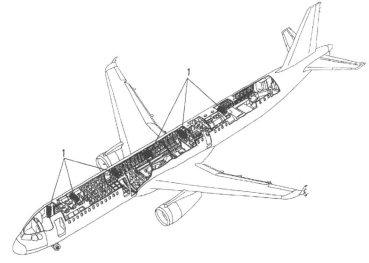

Detection of Signs of Attempted Deception and Other Emotional Stresses by Detecting Changes in Weight Distribution of a Standing or Sitting Person

patent #: US 6852086

This new security device attempts to detect terrorists before they've made it on the plane. It detects "emotional stress" by "measuring variations in the pressure distribution across the subject's footprint". (So much for pogo-sticking through the terminal.)

While I'm suspicious of its accuracy, it does sound much better than alternative methods of detecting deception. The inventors point out that applying "a standard polygraph test to pre-boarding passengers might take several days per airplane". Now that's a long wait!

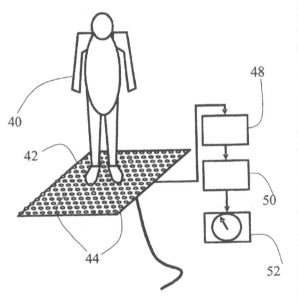

Sanitary Security Sock System

patent #: US 7012525

Anyone who's been on an aeroplane in recent years knows the drill: take off you shoes, put them on the conveyer belt, and walk through the metal detector. All because of that one stupid shoe-bombing m*th#rf!ck%r!

Deep breath in. Deep breath out. Okay. So what's wrong with this shoe X-ray procedure? The inventor points out that "little or no emphasis has been placed on the potential transmission of communicable fungal infections from one passenger to another during the security screening process."

Hmm, I don't want to be blown up, but I'm not too keen on athlete's foot either. What a pickle…

Diane Ghioto's "one size fits all" sock system is protecting the world from the ground up.

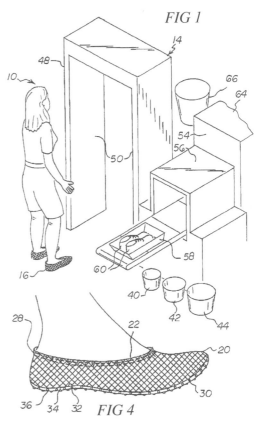

FIG 1

FIG 4

Grenade Cam

patent #: US 6924838

It's a camera on a grenade. Why? So you can see the whites of their eyes as you blow them up from 50 yards away? For recon purposes? "Sir, our cameras show there is an enemy shelter just over the grassy knoll... well there was one anyway. You weren't hoping to take them alive were you?"

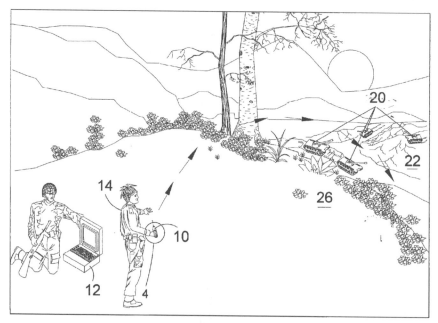

FIG 1

Mobile Bulletproof Personnel Shield

patent #: US 6845701

It seems like new bullets and guns are patented all the time, so it's good to finally see some new armour for a change.

   This shield consists of a bulletproof fabric covering, stretched over a frame. (What a great idea! It could double as camping gear for rappers. Sean John pup tent, anyone?)

   Although the terrain of the shield seems limited by its use of wheels, the inventor points out that due to handicapped access laws, most public buildings are now accessible by ramps and elevators – which should come in handy when trying to subdue the next protest at the old people's home.

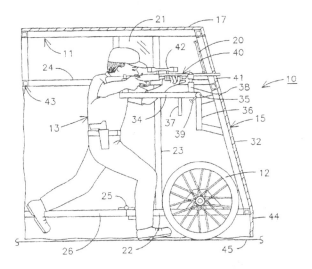

Automated Surveillance Monitor of Non-Humans in Real Time

patent #: US 6782847

The illustrations for this patent go beyond anything I have ever seen.

Tiger, the dog in the foreground, is the front line of defence. Our brave canine (ironically with a feline name) is equipped with a microphone, a video camera and bodily sensors. If he barks at anything suspicious, a signal is sent to a human security guard, who can assess the threat via a camera link.

In the first scenario, Tiger starts barking. False alarm! It's just a little kitty cat. But the next scenario is not so innocent. Masked terrorists storm the facility. Tiger barks. It's the real deal! But our poor doggie, leashed to his post, is gunned down in the line of duty. His heartbeat sensor sends its last signal and a hero is made.

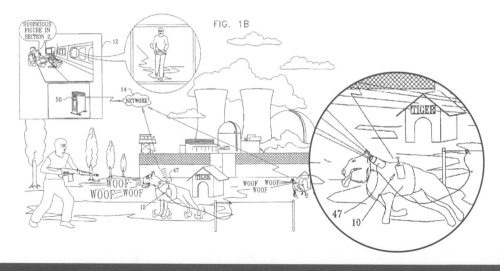

Key Chain Design

patent #: US D520232

Damn, now which cave did I lose
my keys in?

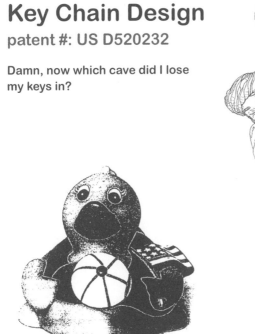

All American Duck

patent #: US D495763

He may spend his winters south of the border, but play the Star Spangled
Banner and this duck's true colours will shine through every time. Would you
spend bath time with a rubber object less patriotic?

Cutter Tool
patent #: US D513578

Box cutters were the weapon of the 9/11 hijackers. How do we prevent another 9/11? If crucifixes are effective against vampires and the Anti-Christ, maybe we should try plastering every box cutter with an American flag? Simple.

Patriotic Themed Duct Tape
patent #: US D513768

Of course, if you were to catch a terrorist and wanted to incapacitate them until the emergency services arrived, you could always bind and gag them with a nice, patriotic length of duct tape.

American Flag Bandage
patent #: US D516730

Nicked you knuckle as you repeatedly "subdued" your terrorist prisoner? Never fear, now you can truly bleed for your country!

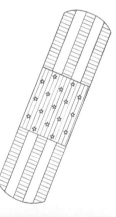

United States of America Shaped Food Product

patent #: US D525411

For a nation of patriotic consumers, what's more exciting than being able to consume your own country!

This design patent assigned to mega-conglomerate Kraft Foods appeals to both proud Americans yearning for some form of national cannibalism ritual, and our Al-Qaeda enemies who would no doubt like to see the nation submerged in boiling water for 8-10 minutes.

Leaders in Washington take note: this greatly simplified, fourteen-state version of the country could do wonders for US national geography scores.

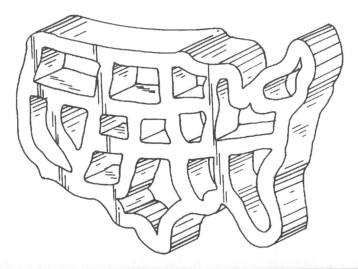

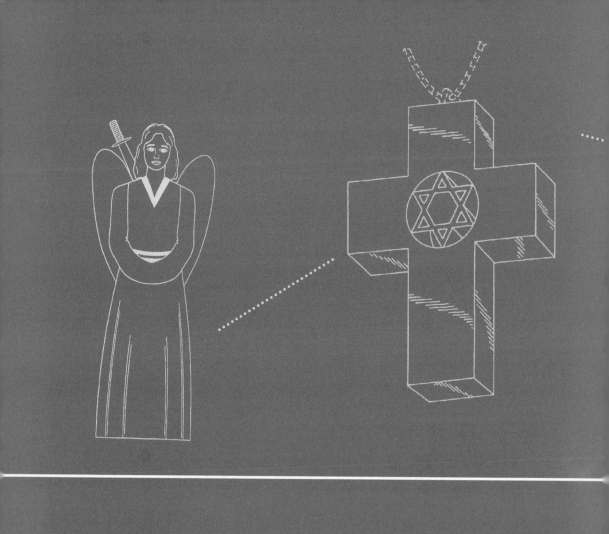

Religion
and Death

Religious Lamp with Fluid Flow
patent #: US 7118242

Jesus said in the book of John (8:12), "I am the light of the world." Now have Him light up your living room!

But this Jesus lamp does a little more than just light up. When you turn Him on, "Jesus' head rises". He reincarnates on command!

And the spiritual uplift doesn't end there. There is also a "fluid flow system" that "circulates simulated blood out through the body of Jesus", dripping out for that I-can't-believe-how-much-this-guy-suffered-for-me effect. Holy shit.

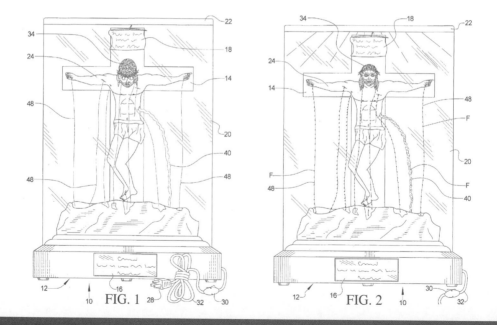

FIG. 1   FIG. 2

Religious Display Sign

patent #: US D516631

Just in case your vocabulary doesn't include the word "church"…

Female Doll Resembling an Angel

patent #: US D491236

Never talk to an angel with a giant sword and no halo.

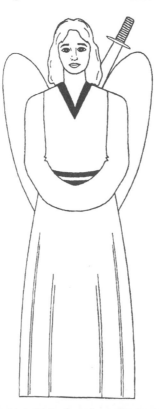

Cross

patent #: US D522403

The owner of this design patent wants us to know he did it for us. But Marcus McIver of Oakland Park, Florida, I don't even know you!

Cross USB Drive

patent #: US D533179

Jesus saves and He backs up.

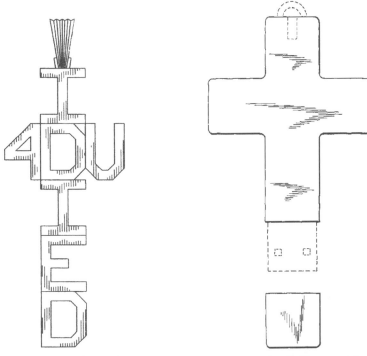

Peanut-Shaped Prayer Cushion

patent #: US
6810541

"New use" patents are a little strange. Essentially, they are issued for new uses of existing technology.

For example, this inventor admits that peanut-shaped cushions have been patented and that knee cushions have been patented. But never have the two been combined in the service of the Lord. Hallelujah! We have a new patent!

10

Fig. 1

Religious Meditation Apparatus

patent #: US 6837185

According to the inventor, "[a] need has existed for a meditation tool that also acts as a bird feeder so that watching the birds can enhance a religious experience."

Also it's an ingenious way to convert birds to the faith! While they're enjoying a nice free meal, why not remind them that Christ died for their sins, too. After all, where were they during the whole Crucifixion? A few woodpeckers could have prevented the whole debacle.

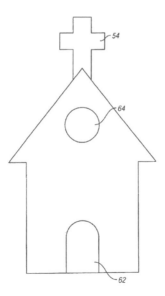

Travel Toothbrush with Dental Cream Included

patent #: US 6793433

Inventing is a mysterious process: who knows where true inspiration comes from? Inventor Juan David Giraldo credits the Big Guy in the Sky:

> I thank God for giving me the opportunity to create this invention for the well-being of humanity.

And God said, "Let toothbrush and toothpaste no longer be divided!" And behold, they were one.

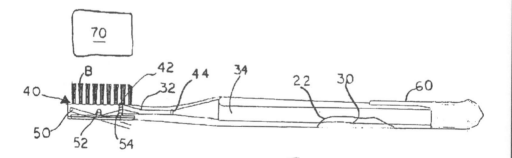

Medal

patent #: US D517445

Christian Cross

patent #: US D506945

Many a designer has asked, "Can't we all just get along?"

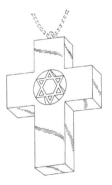

Alpha Star Cross Omega Design

patent #: US D528939

Seasonal Multicultural Hat

patent #: US D501980

Even just for Christmas?

Combination Lawn/Garden Ornament and Cremation Container

patent #: US 6854165

I suppose there are worse lawn ornaments in which to spend eternity (Pink flamingo, anyone?). It's still a little bit odd though.

What's that creepy sound coming from the porch? That's just grandpa.

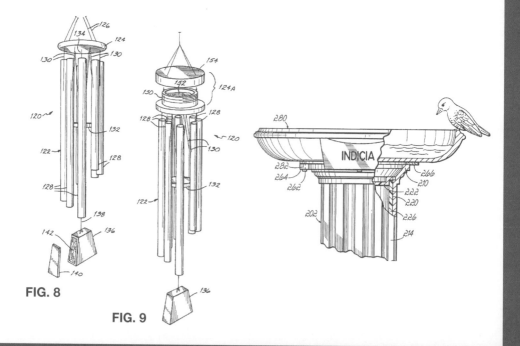

FIG. 8

FIG. 9

Vehicle Shaped Caskets and Urns

patent #: US 6763558

If you're the type of car fanatic that likes to spend time under the bonnet, you might want to cruise the highway to heaven in this "Vehicle Shaped Casket". Just make sure you've lined up some really strong pallbearers!

Unfortunately it doesn't have reverse.

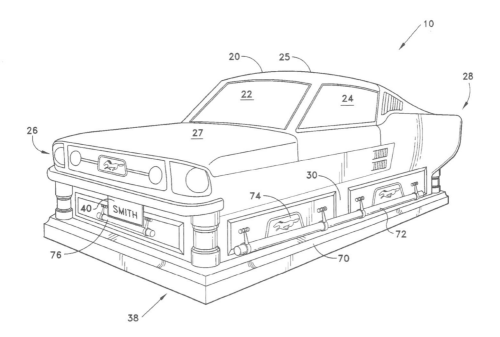

Baseball Bat Urn

patent #: US D524510

If you've always wanted to "go out swinging", once you're gone why not be the one swung? With this sporty urn you will not only be able to attend your grandchildren's baseball games, but you'll also be a part of the action.

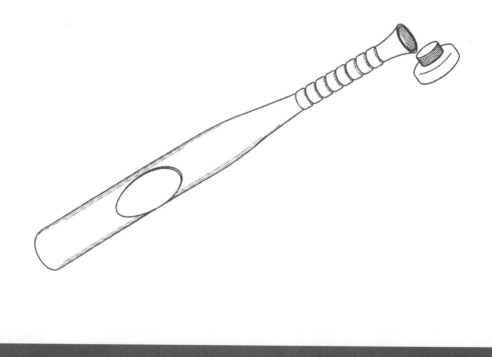

Funeral Flag

patent #: US D527306

It's a flag. It says "Funeral". It's a Funeral Flag. Design Patent granted.

Burial Structure for the Interment of Human Remains and Significant Memorabilia

patent #: US 6799399

Hmm, this looks like something I've seen before… Oh, yeah, the pyramids of Egypt that were built 4,000 years ago. Some modifications were made and a patent was issued. Good luck collecting royalties from the Pharaohs!

While constructing a pyramid might stretch your budget, you could probably afford to be a brick in this one. Wedged in here, you will be "kept safe from vandals and other intrudes [*sic*]."

The patent is full of interesting information about developments in burial practices. Did you know Abraham Lincoln and John Dillinger are buried beneath several feet of concrete to discourage grave robbers? Fascinating.

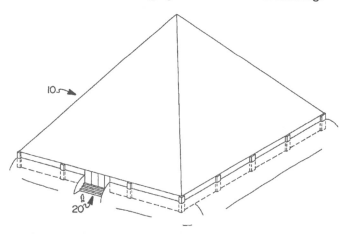

Artificial Underwater Memorializing Catacomb and Reef System

patent #: US 7024735

If you love water and jigsaw puzzles, there's never been a better time to die. When it comes to death care, inventor Morris Huggins thinks outside the box.

In Huggins' system, your cremated remains are embedded in a concrete container, which can interlock with other containers to create large-scale works. In death, you can provide a habitat for sealife, create catacombs for adventurous divers and be part of a giant "Crucifix, Star of David, or Army insignia" for your relatives to enjoy from the comfort of a glass-bottomed boat.

The patent boasts that the "unique combination of an underwater theme park[!], artificial reef, catacomb system and memorial creates an ambiance heretofore unparalleled." First stop, Disney World. Second stop Grandma and Grandpa's Adventure Columbarium!

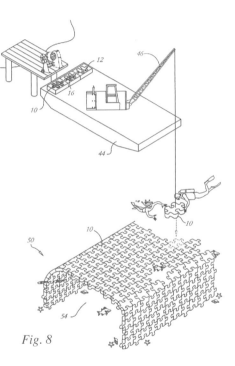

Fig. 8

Acknowledgements

This book is the culmination of years of research and writing that began with the Patently Silly website (www.patentlysilly.com). I have many friends and colleagues to thank for helping me along this trip:

- Cy Adler, man of big ideas, who's enriched the lives of all those willing to take the ride.
- Alex Eben Meyer, collaborator extraordinaire, who made Patently Silly look cool.
- Gareth Jones for making this book happen.
- Ed Martin, Robert Stein and Ben Eisman for their knowledge of legalese.
- Paul Godwin, Danielle Svetcov, Ginger and Frances Park, Carrie McLaren and Charles Star for excellent advice.
- My fellow patent bloggers out there who made PS legit.
- Jen Nails, Nick Kroll, Rachel Parenta, Kurt and Kristen, Andres du Bouchet and Carl Fink for helping the Patently Silly live show get moving.
- Aunt Tracey, Sean Pangia, Jasmine Nielsen, Matthew Simonelli, Tobin Brogunier, Dawn Falato, Noah Davis, Joe Beshenkovsky and Ben Strawbridge for all-around awesomeness.
- Grandma Margaret who I know would carry this book in her purse at all times.
- Mom and Dad for everything else.
- Nathan and Larissa are chumps!

This whole endeavour would not be possible without:

- The men and women of the USPTO who are patently cool.
- And of course, the inventors and patent illustrators of the world, without whom this would just be a book of empty pages.

£2.00

D0655427

The Houseplant
Almanac

Christine Walkden

Bloomsbury Books · London

To all those who help me when I need it most.
You know who you are.

First published by Lochar Publishing Ltd.
Moffat, Scotland DG10 9ED.

This edition published by Bloomsbury Books, an imprint of
The Godfrey Cave Group, 42 Bloomsbury Street, London, WC1B 3QJ,
under licence from Eric Dobby Publishing Ltd,
12 Warnford Road, Orpington, Kent BR6 6LW, 1993

Copyright © Christine Walkden, 1992.

Printed and bound in Great Britain by
BPCC Hazell Books Ltd
Member of BPCC Ltd

ISBN 1 85471 391 4

Contents

Acknowledgements

I would like to express my sincere thanks to George Brown and Lochar Publishing and their staff for making this book possible.

Hilary Course not only allowed me to use her word processor for this publication, but taught me how to use it in the process of my writing the book. Her patience, kindness and encouragement were all necessary and most gratefully received.

Two nurseries allowed me to photograph their plants. At the Dutch Nursery at Bell Bar, Hatfield, Herts, I thank the Hen family for great freedom and assistance. Thanks also to Rochfords at Crews Hill for pulling back the thermal screens when necessary.

Christine M. Walkden
October 1991

Introduction

Houseplants are becoming increasingly popular in today's homes, not only for their beauty but also because they are thought to act as air filters and to improve the atmosphere by absorbing unwanted gases.

However, I still find that most houseplants are killed through over-watering, under-watering or putting them in the wrong place.

This publication is intended to provide a succinct and simple guide, answering all the basic questions asked by the gardener, enabling him or her to maintain the plants in good condition over many years.

Feeding of most houseplants should take place throughout the growing season. This means from April through to late September. Once light levels start to decline in the autumn, the plants' growth naturally slows down, and their requirement for fertilizer stops. Feeding beyond September can result in very soft growth which is prone to pest and disease attack and the production of leaves at the expense of flowers.

For flowering plants feeding with a potash-rich fertilizer is ideal. This can either be bought as a potash-rich houseplant fertilizer or as a tomato fertilizer. Note the manufacturers' instructions for application rates and frequency unless otherwise stated in the text.

Houseplants can be grown by anyone, even the person who has never grown a plant before. If you happen to kill one or two on the path to success, do not be put off. The only real way to learn how to grow your plants is by growing them, using the tips in this book to help you gain the necessary experience.

May I wish you many happy hours caring for and enjoying some of the plants detailed in this guide.

Flowering Plants
for Well-Lit
Positions

Common names	Hot water plants, Cupid's bower.
Botanical name	*Achimenes* 'Rosy Red'.
Interesting facts	Name probably from the Greek, meaning not surviving the winter, being frost sensitive. Also thought to be named after King Hakhamash of Turkey.
Origin	Tropical areas of America and Mexico.
Position	Well-lit but away from direct sun in summer.
Temperature	Minimum winter temperature 55F.
Watering	Use tepid water to keep compost moist at all times during growing season. Once flowering stops allow to dry, cut off stems and store rhizomes in dry peat over winter.
Feeding	Every 2 weeks throughout growing season with potash-rich house plant fertilizer.
Humidity	Do not wet leaves. Stand pots on damp gravel tray and keep moist at all times.
Re-potting	Re-pot rhizomes into fresh compost in early spring.
Propagation	From rhizomes or stem cuttings taken in May.

Common name	African lilies.
Botanical name	*Agapanthus.*
Interesting facts	Name derived from Greek, *agape,* love and *anthos,* a flower.
Origin	South Africa.
Position	Full sun.
Temperature	Minimum winter temperature of 40–45F.
Watering	Maintain dampness in the compost throughout growing season. From November to early April give very little water.
Feeding	During growing season with potash-rich fertilizer.
Humidity	Misting is not necessary.
Re-potting	Not required until division takes place.
Propagation	Divide plant every 4–5 years.

Common name	Belladonna lily.
Botanical name	*Amaryllis belladonna.*
Interesting facts	Named after a shepherdess mentioned in Theocritus and Virgil, Greek and Latin poets.
Origin	South Africa.
Position	Full sun.
Temperature	Minimum winter temperature of 50F.
Watering	Start watering when growth begins. Allow compost surface to dry out between waterings.
Feeding	During growing season with potash-rich fertilizer.
Humidity	Mist leaves occasionally.
Re-potting	Every 3–5 years.
Propagation	Offsets at re-potting time.

Common name	Wax Begonia.
Botanical name	*Begonia semperflorens.*
Interesting facts	The specific name *semperflorens* means 'always flowering'.
Origin	Brazil.
Position	Bright light but not direct sunlight.
Temperature	Not less than 55F in winter.
Watering	Compost should be moist throughout growing season, but allow surface to dry out between waterings.
Feeding	Throughout growing season with potash-rich fertilizer.
Humidity	Mist leaves frequently, but never wet the flowers. Stand pots on gravel trays.
Re-potting	Normally thrown away after flowering as they are treated as annuals.
Propagation	From seed sown in spring.

Common name	Begonia.
Botanical name	*Begonia tuberhybrida.*
Interesting facts	Tuberous hybrids derived mainly from *B. boliviensis, B. pearcei* and *B. rosaeflora.*
Origin	Garden origin.
Position	Well-lit position away from direct sun.
Temperature	Minimum winter temperature 55F.
Watering	Water frequently when plant is in flower. Compost should not however be constantly soggy.
Feeding	Feed regularly throughout growing season with potash-rich fertilizer.
Humidity	Mist plants frequently and surround pots with damp compost or peat.
Re-potting	Normally tuber is thrown away after flowering, or dried off, stored over winter in peat and potted in spring.
Propagation	Pot tubers in spring.

Common name	Shrimp plant.
Botanical name	*Beloperone guttata.*
Interesting facts	*Beloperone* is derived from the Greek *belos*, an arrow and *perone*, a buckle – a reference to the way the anther lobes are connected.
Origin	Mexico.
Position	Well-lit, with some direct light.
Temperature	Minimum winter temperature 45F.
Watering	Water well throughout growing season but sparingly in winter.
Feeding	Throughout growing season with potash-rich fertilizer.
Humidity	Mist leaves occasionally.
Re-potting	Re-pot in spring if necessary.
Propagation	Stem cuttings.

Common name	Paper flower.
Botanical name	*Bougainvillea x buttiana* 'Brilliant'.
Interesting facts	Named after French navigator who sailed around the world in 1767-69, Louis Antoine de Bougainville.
Origin	A hybrid between *B. glabra* and *B. peruviana*.
Position	Full sun.
Temperature	Minimum winter temperature 45F.
Watering	Water well throughout growing season, keeping compost almost dry in winter.
Feeding	Throughout season with potash-rich fertilizer.
Humidity	Mist frequently if grown in heated room.
Re-potting	Only if essential in the spring.
Propagation	Stem cuttings in summer.

Common name	Bush violet.
Botanical name	*Browallia speciosa* 'Blue Troll'.
Interesting facts	The plant is thought to be named after J. Browallius, Bishop of Abo, Sweden, who was also a botanist.
Origin	Colombia.
Position	Bright light with some direct sun.
Temperature	Minimum winter temperature 50F.
Watering	Compost should be moist throughout growing season.
Feeding	Throughout season with potash-rich fertilizer.
Humidity	Mist leaves occasionally.
Re-potting	Normally grown as an annual and thrown away after flowering.
Propagation	Sow seeds in spring or summer.

Common names	The slipper flower, Pocket book plant.
Botanical name	*Calceolaria x herbeohybrida*.
Interesting facts	Named after F. Calceolari, 16th-century Italian botanist.
Origin	Garden hybrid.
Position	Bright, but away from direct light.
Temperature	Cool, between 50–60F.
Watering	Compost should be moist at all times.
Feeding	Throughout growing season with potash-rich fertilizer.
Humidity	Do not mist leaves or flowers, but stand pots on a pebble tray and keep moist.
Re-potting	Normally seed grown, pricked out into 3.5 inch pots, then into 5 inch pots.
Propagation	By seed in summer in a cool greenhouse for flowering the following year. Throw plants away after flowering.

Common name	Bottlebrush plant.
Botanical name	*Callistemon citrinus.*
Interesting facts	From the Greek *kallistos*, beautiful, and *stemon*, a stamen. The beauty of the flower is the bright red stamens. The foliage is lemon-scented.
Origin	Australia and New Caledonia.
Position	Good well-lit position, but out of direct sunlight.
Temperature	Minimum winter temperature 45F.
Watering	Water well from spring until autumn, then keep on the dry side throughout the winter.
Feeding	From April–September with a potash-rich fertilizer.
Humidity	Misting is not necessary.
Re-potting	Re-pot when necessary in late April.
Propagation	Stem cuttings in the spring.

Common names	Italian bellflower, Star of Bethlehem, The Bell Flower.
Botanical name	*Campanula isophylla.*
Interesting facts	Name derived from the Latin for 'a little bell'.
Origin	North-west Italy.
Position	Well-lit spot, but avoid direct sun in summer.
Temperature	Minimum winter temperature of 45F.
Watering	Keep compost moist during the growing season, but reduce amount in winter months.
Feeding	Throughout growing season with potash-rich fertilizer.
Humidity	Occasionally mist the leaves.
Re-potting	Re-pot every spring.
Propagation	Stem cuttings in spring. Seed in the spring or division at re-potting.

Common names	Pot mum, Florist's chrysanthemum.
Botanical name	*Chrysanthemum morifolium.*
Interesting facts	Named after the Greek *chrysos*, gold, and *anthos*, a flower.
Origin	From China in 1764.
Position	Good bright light is necessary but plants should be shaded from midday sun.
Temperature	Cool, between 50–60F, especially when in flower to extend flowering.
Watering	Plants should be moist at all times.
Feeding	Throughout growing season with potash-rich fertilizer.
Humidity	Mist leaves occasionally.
Re-potting	Normally not necessary as plant is sold just before flowering.
Propagation	Due to cultural techniques employed by the professional to dwarf the plants, it is not easy for the amateur to produce good results.

Common names	Parrot's bill, Koka beak, Lobster claw, Glory pea.
Botanical name	*Clianthus puniceus 'Albus'.*
Interesting facts	Name derived from the Greek meaning 'Glory flower'.
Origin	New Zealand.
Position	Full sun.
Temperature	Minimum winter temperature 50F.
Watering	Water well from spring until autumn, letting the compost surface dry slightly between waterings. During winter water sparingly.
Feeding	Throughout growing season with balanced plant fertilizer.
Humidity	Mist leaves on warm days or stand on a gravel tray.
Re-potting	Re-pot when necessary in the spring.
Propagation	Sow seeds in the spring. Stem cuttings in the summer.

Common name	The Kaffir lily.
Botanical name	*Clivia miniata.*
Interesting facts	Named after a Duchess of Northumberland, Lady Charlotte Florentina Clive, who died in 1868.
Origin	Warm dry forests of South Africa.
Position	Bright light, but avoid direct sun in summer as it may scorch the leaves.
Temperature	Minimum winter temperature of 40–50F. This is necessary for the flower to form.
Watering	Water lightly from late autumn to early spring until the flower spike is 6 inches high, then water well ensuring that entire root ball is moist.
Feeding	Do not feed during winter months, thereafter use a house plant fertilizer rich in potash.
Humidity	Sponge leaves occasionally to remove dust and freshen plant.
Re-potting	After flowering, and only when roots have absolutely filled the pot.
Propagation	By division at time of re-potting.

Common name	Firecracker flower.
Botanical name	*Crossandra undulifolia (infundibuliformis).*
Interesting facts	Name derived from Greek, *krossus*, a fringe, and *aner*, male, referring to the fringed anthers. *Undulifolia* means wavy foliage.
Origin	India, Sri Lanka.
Position	Well-lit position but avoid direct light in summer.
Temperature	Minimum winter temperature of 55F.
Watering	During the growing season the compost should be moist all the time. Reduce the amount in winter.
Feeding	Throughout growing season with potash-rich fertilizer once a week.
Humidity	Stand pots on damp gravel tray and keep atmosphere moist.
Re-potting	Only re-pot if necessary in the spring before flowering.
Propagation	Stem cuttings in the summer or seed in the spring.

Common name	Crown of thorns.
Botanical name	*Euphorbia milii splendens.*
Interesting facts	The sap is poisonous so keep away from eyes and mouth. Named after Euphorbus, physician to Juba, King of Mauritania.
Origin	Madagascar. *E. milii* is said to be named after M. Millius, governor of the Isle of Bourbon.
Position	Well-lit but shade from direct sun in summer.
Temperature	Minimum winter temperature 55F.
Watering	Water moderately during growing season, letting surface of compost dry between waterings. Reduce frequency in the winter months.
Feeding	Every 2 weeks from April–September with a potash-rich fertilizer.
Humidity	Misting is not necessary.
Re-potting	Re-pot every second spring if necessary.
Propagation	Stem cuttings in June and July. Allow milky sap to dry before placing in compost.

23

Common name	Poinsettia.
Botanical name	*Euphorbia pulcherrima.*
Interesting facts	Introduced in 1834 and named in honour of the Mexican traveller and American Minister to Mexico, Joel Roberts Poinsett, who first found the plant in 1828.
Origin	Native of Mexico and tropical America.
Position	Maximum light is necessary during winter; sunny position during summer months but out of direct sun.
Temperature	Minimum winter temperature of 55–60F.
Watering	Water well during the flowering season so that the entire pot is wet.
Feeding	From July feed weekly with potash-rich houseplant fertilizer.
Humidity	Mist leaves frequently during the flowering season.
Re-potting	Not normally necessary as the plant is generally bought in flower and normally thrown away after flowering.
Propagation	Stem cuttings in early summer. Not widely practised by the home gardener.

Common name	Fuchsia.
Botanical name	*Fuchsia tripyhlla* 'Gartenmeister Bonstedt'.
Interesting facts	Named after the 14th-century German botanist Leonard Fuchs.
Origin	Haiti, San Domingo.
Position	Bright light away from direct sun.
Temperature	Minimum winter temperature 55F.
Watering	Water well during growing season keeping compost moist. Water sparingly during winter.
Feeding	Throughout growing season with potash-rich fertilizer.
Humidity	Mist leaves frequently during summer. Stand pots on damp gravel trays.
Re-potting	Re-pot every year in the spring.
Propagation	Softwood cuttings in spring.

Common names	Blood lily, Red Cape.
Botanical name	*Haemanthus natalensis.*
Interesting facts	Name derived from the Greek, *haima*, meaning blood, (alluding to the red colour of the flower), and *anthos*, a flower.
Origin	Natal, South Africa.
Position	Full sun.
Temperature	Minimum winter temperature 55F.
Watering	Compost must never be very wet, while during the winter it should be on the dry side.
Feeding	Throughout the growing season with potash-rich fertilizer.
Humidity	Place plants on a gravel tray and keep moist.
Re-potting	Only when necessary.
Propagation	Divide offsets at re-potting stage.

Common names	Heliotrope, Cherry pie.
Botanical name	*Heliotropium peruvianum (H. arborescens).*
Interesting facts	Name derived from the Greek *helios*, the sun, and *trope*, to turn. An old belief has it that the flowers turn to the sun.
Origin	Peru.
Position	Well-lit position but shade from hot sun.
Temperature	Minimum winter temperature 40F.
Watering	Keep compost damp at all times. Reduce watering in the winter.
Feeding	Throughout growing season with potash-rich fertilizer.
Humidity	Mist occasionally.
Re-potting	Re-pot every year in the spring.
Propagation	Stem cutting in summer.

Common names	Guinea gold vine, Snake vine.
Botanical name	*Hibbertia scandens.*
Interesting facts	Named after a patron of botany, George Hibbert, who had a botanic garden at Clapham.
Origin	Queensland, New South Wales.
Position	Full sun.
Temperature	Minimum winter temperature 50F.
Watering	Water well throughout growing season, but allow compost to dry out between waterings.
Feeding	Throughout growing season with potash-rich fertilizer.
Humidity	Mist leaves occasionally or stand pots on damp gravel tray.
Re-potting	Re-pot when necessary in the spring.
Propagation	By seed or layering in the spring, or by cuttings in the summer.

Common name	Rose of China.
Botanical name	*Hibiscus rosa-sinensis.*
Interesting facts	*Hibiscus* is a Greek name of a very ancient origin used by the poet Virgil for a marrow-like plant.
Origin	Tropics and sub-tropics.
Position	Good well-lit position but out of direct sunlight.
Temperature	Minimum winter temperature 55F.
Watering	Keep moist at all times, but reduce slightly during the winter months.
Feeding	From April to September with a balanced houseplant fertilizer.
Humidity	Mist leaves occasionally or stand plants on a damp gravel tray.
Re-potting	May be necessary yearly in April.
Propagation	Stem cuttings in late spring.

Common name	Amaryllis.
Botanical name	*Hippeastrum hybrida.*
Interesting facts	From Greek, *hippeus,* a knight and *astron,* a star.
Origin	Central and South America.
Position	Full sun.
Temperature	Minimum winter temperature 50F.
Watering	Start watering when growth begins. Allow compost surface to dry out between waterings.
Feeding	During growing season with potash-rich fertilizer.
Humidity	Mist leaves occasionally.
Re-potting	Every 3–5 years.
Propagation	Offsets at re-potting time.

Common names	Chinese jasmine, Pink jasmine.
Botanical name	*Jasminum polyanthum.*
Interesting facts	Extremely fragrant flowers in the spring. *Polyanthum* means 'many flowered'. The name *Jasminum* is said to be derived from *ysmyn,* an Arabic name for jasmine.
Origin	Western China.
Position	Well-lit position with some direct light.
Temperature	Minimum winter temperature 45F.
Watering	Keep compost moist at all times.
Feeding	Throughout growing season with potash-rich fertilizer.
Humidity	Mist leaves often and stand pots on a damp gravel tray.
Re-potting	Re-pot when necessary.
Propagation	By stem cuttings in the spring.

Common name	Flaming Katy.
Botanical name	*Kalanchoe blossfeldiana.*
Interesting facts	*Kalanchoe* is the Latinized form of the Chinese name of one species.
Origin	Malagasy.
Position	During growing season in east - or west-facing windowsill, during the winter months on a south-facing windowsill.
Temperature	Minimum winter temperature of 50F.
Watering	Water well, but allow surface of compost to dry out between waterings.
Feeding	Throughout growing season with potash-rich fertilizer.
Humidity	This plant will tolerate a dry atmosphere.
Re-potting	Every year in the spring.
Propagation	From seeds or cuttings in the spring.

Common name	Kalanchoe.
Botanical name	*Kalanchoe uniflora (Bryophyllum uniflorum).*
Interesting facts	*Kalanchoe* is the Latinized form of the Chinese name for one species, and *uniflora* means one-flowered.
Origin	Malagasy.
Position	Full sun.
Temperature	Minimum winter temperature 55F.
Watering	Water thoroughly, then allow compost surface to dry before watering again. Reduce watering in winter.
Feeding	Feed throughout growing season with potash-rich fertilizer.
Humidity	This plant can tolerate a dry atmosphere.
Re-potting	Re-pot in spring after the plant's winter rest.
Propagation	From seed.

Common name	Cape cowslip.
Botanical name	*Lachenalia aloides (L. tricolor).*
Interesting facts	Named after Werner de la Chenal, Professor of Botany at Basle University.
Origin	Cape.
Position	Well-lit with some full sun.
Temperature	Minimum winter temperature of 45F.
Watering	Keep compost moist at all times during flowering and continue for several weeks, then gradually reduce amount and stop.
Feeding	Feed with potash-rich fertilizer throughout growing season.
Humidity	Mist leaves occasionally.
Re-potting	Re-pot every September.
Propagation	Remove offsets and re-plant in September.

Common name	Banana.
Botanical name	*Musa.*
Interesting facts	The name is of doubtful origin, possibly honouring Antonius Musa, a freedman of Emperor Augustus. The Arabic and Egyptian name is Mauz and this is considered by some to be the basis of the Latin *Musa*.
Origin	Tropical Asia and East Africa.
Position	Well-lit but out of direct sunlight.
Temperature	Minimum winter temperature of 66F.
Watering	During growing season ensure that compost is moist at all times. During winter allow the surface to dry before watering again.
Feeding	With a well-balanced fertilizer throughout the growing season.
Humidity	Occasionally mist the leaves.
Re-potting	When necessary.
Propagation	By division, offsets or suckers when potting or by seed in spring.

Common names	Oleander, Rose-bay.
Botanical name	*Nerium oleander.*
Interesting facts	*Nerium* is the ancient Greek name for oleander. This plant contains poisonous sap but has fragrant flowers.
Origin	Mediterranean region, across Asia to Japan.
Position	Full sun.
Temperature	Minimum winter temperature of 45F.
Watering	Water well during the growing season, but just keep damp in the winter months.
Feeding	Throughout growing season with potash-rich fertilizer.
Humidity	Do not mist leaves. This plant will tolerate a dry atmosphere.
Re-potting	Re-pot when necessary in the spring.
Propagation	Stem cuttings in the spring or summer or from seeds in the spring.

Common names	Passion flower, Banana passion fruits.
Botanical name	*Passiflora exonensis.*
Interesting facts	*Passiflora* derives from the Latin *passio,* passion and *flos,* a flower. From the linking of the flower, by Jesuit missionaries, to the Passion of Christ.
Origin	Garden origin. A hybrid between *P. antioquiensis x mollissima.*
Position	Full sun.
Temperature	Minimum winter temperature 40–50F.
Watering	Daily watering may be necessary in the summer to keep the compost moist. Reduce the amount during winter.
Feeding	Throughout the growing season with a potash-rich fertilizer.
Humidity	Mist leaves occasionally.
Re-potting	When necessary.
Propagation	Cuttings in the spring.

Common name	Geranium.
Botanical name	*Pelargonium hortorum* hybrid.
Interesting facts	Seed head is said to resemble the head of a stork. Greek *pelargos*, a stork.
Origin	Africa, Atlantic Islands, eastwards to Arabia and South India, also in Australasia.
Position	Direct sunlight is necessary for good growth.
Temperature	Minimum winter temperature of 45F.
Watering	Water well, then leave compost to dry between waterings. During winter keep compost barely moist.
Feeding	From April to September with a potash-rich fertilizer.
Humidity	Misting is not necessary and may cause petal marking if carried out when the plant is in flower.
Re-potting	When necessary in the spring.
Propagation	Stem tip cuttings in the spring and summer. Do not use hormone rooting compounds.

Common names	Cape leadwort, Blue Cape.
Botanical name	*Plumbago capensis.*
Interesting facts	*Plumbago* from the Latin *plumbum*, lead, named by the Roman Pliny who attributed the curing of lead disease to the European species.
Origin	Widespread in the warmer regions of the world.
Position	Bright well-lit position with some direct light.
Temperature	Minimum winter temperature of 45F.
Watering	During the growing season keep the compost moist at all times. Water sparingly in the winter.
Feeding	From April to September with a general liquid fertilizer.
Humidity	Mist frequently.
Re-potting	When necessary in the spring.
Propagation	Seed sown in the spring or stem cuttings in the autumn.

Common names	Poor man's orchid, Butterfly flower.
Botanical name	*Schizanthus* hybrida.
Interesting facts	From the Greek, *schizo*, to cut, and *anthos*, a flower. The flowers have deeply fringed petals.
Origin	Garden hybrid.
Position	Well-lit in direct sun.
Temperature	Minimum winter temperature of 50–60F.
Watering	Keep moist at all times.
Feeding	From April to September with a potash-rich fertilizer.
Humidity	Mist leaves occasionally or stand on damp gravel tray.
Re-potting	Normally grown as annuals and thrown away after flowering.
Propagation	Sow seed in the spring or autumn.

Common name	Cineraria.
Botanical name	*Senecio cruentus.*
Interesting facts	Name derived from Latin *cinereus* meaning ash - coloured, referring to the colour of the underside of the leaves.
Origin	Derived from species of *senecio* introduced during the 18th century from the Canaries.
Position	Bright light away from direct sunshine.
Temperature	45–55F is best to ensure long flowering period.
Watering	Water frequently with tepid water.
Feeding	8 weeks after potting start to feed with potash-rich fertilizer.·
Humidity	Stand pot on saucer of pebbles and keep these moist.
Re-potting	Normally seed produced, pricked out, moved to 3.5 inch pot, then to 5 inch pot.
Propagation	Seed raised in May through to July in cool greenhouse.

Common names	Jacobean lily, Aztec lily.
Botanical name	*Sprekelia formosissima (Amaryllis formosissima).*
Interesting facts	Named after J. H. von Sprekelsen, a German lawyer, who sent the plant to Linnaeus, the person who classified plants.
Origin	Mexico.
Position	Well-lit.
Temperature	Minimum winter temperature of 45–50F.
Watering	Dry off leaves in autumn when they start going yellow. Plant in late winter or early spring leaving neck of bulb just above soil surface.
Feeding	Use balanced houseplant fertilizer in the spring.
Humidity	Place pots on a damp gravel tray.
Re-potting	In late winter or early spring.
Propagation	By offsets or seed.

Common name	Cape primrose.
Botanical name	*Streptocarpus* 'Lady Strathallen'.
Interesting facts	Name derived from Greek, *streptos,* twisted, and *karpos,* a fruit which is spiralled.
Origin	Garden hybrid.
Position	Brightly-lit spot away from direct sun in summer.
Temperature	Minimum winter temperature of 55F.
Watering	Water freely, but allow compost surface to dry between waterings. Water sparingly in winter.
Feeding	Every 2 weeks from April to September with potash-rich fertilizer.
Humidity	Stand plants on a damp gravel tray.
Re-potting	Re-pot every spring.
Propagation	Divide plants in the spring or take leaf sections cuttings in the summer. May also be raised from seed sown in the spring.

Common name	Black-eyed Susan.
Botanical name	*Thunbergia alata* 'Susie'.
Interesting facts	The plant is named after the Swedish botanist Karl P. Thunber who was a student of Linnaeus and travelled widely in South Africa.
Origin	Tropical Africa.
Position	A well-lit position in full sun.
Temperature	Minimum winter temperature of 55F.
Watering	Keep the compost moist at all times.
Feeding	Throughout growing season with a potash-rich fertilizer.
Humidity	Mist frequently and stand pot on damp gravel tray.
Re-potting	Normally grown as an annual and thrown away after flowering.
Propagation	From seed in early spring.

Common name	Yellow arum lily.
Botanical name	*Zantedeschia* 'Lady Luck'.
Interesting facts	Named after the Italian botanist Francesco Zantedischi.
Origin	Garden hybrid.
Position	A well-lit position with some direct light.
Temperature	Minimum winter temperature of 50F.
Watering	During the growing season keep the compost wet at all times.
Feeding	During the growing season with potash-rich fertilizer.
Humidity	Mist leaves occasionally.
Re-potting	After flowering reduce water and then stop altogether when the foliage turns yellow. Re-pot into fresh compost in the autumn.
Propagation	Division of the rhizome or pot up offsets at re-potting in the autumn.

Foliage Plants
for Well-Lit Positions

Common names	Century plant, Maguey.
Botanical name	*Agave americana medio-picta.*
Interesting facts	The sap is fermented to produce the Mexican national drink pulque.
Origin	Mexico.
Position	Full sun especially in winter.
Temperature	Minimum winter temperature of 45F.
Watering	Water like a normal houseplant during the summer, in the autumn reduce the amount and by October keep almost dry.
Feeding	Feed with a balanced houseplant fertilizer from May to August.
Humidity	Do not mist and give plenty of ventilation.
Re-potting	Only when necessary.
Propagation	Seed sown in the spring, re-pot divisions when necessary.

Common name	Common pineapple.
Botanical name	*Ananas comosus variegatus.*
Interesting facts	Name derived from South American name for pineapple – *nanas.*
Origin	Tropics of Central and South America.
Position	Full sun.
Temperature	Minimum winter temperature of 50F.
Watering	Never over-water and ensure there is good drainage, but keep compost moist.
Feeding	Every 2 weeks with potash-rich fertilizer.
Humidity	Mist leaves occasionally, or stand plant on damp gravel tray.
Re-potting	Only when pot-bound.
Propagation	By offsets, from base of plant.

Common name	Iron Cross Begonia.
Botanical name	*Begonia masoniana.*
Interesting facts	Named after Mr L. Maurice Mason. Common name is said to refer to the brown pattern on the leaf which resembles the German Iron Cross.
Origin	South-East Asia.
Position	A well-lit position out of direct sunlight. Turn plant frequently to prevent one-sided growth.
Temperature	Minimum winter temperature of 55F.
Watering	Keep compost moist from April to October then reduce over winter, allowing surface of compost to dry between waterings.
Feeding	Feed from April to October with a balanced houseplant fertilizer.
Humidity	A moist atmosphere is essential or brown leaf margins occur. Stand plant on a damp gravel tray and mist leaves frequently.
Re-potting	Re-pot each spring if necessary.
Propagation	By division.

Common names	Flame nettle, Painted nettle.
Botanical name	*Coleus blumei.*
Interesting facts	Name derived from the Greek *koleos*, a sheath, referring to the stamens being united to enclose the style. Named after Carl Ludwig von Blume.
Origin	Tropical Africa and Asia.
Position	Well-lit position but out of direct sunlight.
Temperature	Minimum winter temperature of 50F.
Watering	During growing season keep moist at all times, reduce watering in the winter.
Feeding	Feed with a nitrogen-rich fertilizer from April to September.
Humidity	Maintain a moist atmosphere at all times. Stand plant on a damp gravel tray.
Re-potting	Cut back growth in February or March and re-pot each season.
Propagation	Sow seeds in February or March or from stem cutting in spring or summer.

Common name	Jade plant.
Botanical name	*Crassula argentea (C.portulacea).*
Interesting facts	Name derived from the Latin *crassus,* thick. referring to the thick or fleshy leaves of the plant.
Origin	Nomaqualand to Transvaal.
Position	Well-lit but out of direct sunlight.
Temperature	Minimum winter temperature of 45F.
Watering	Water well throughout growing season, but keep on the dry side during winter.
Feeding	Throughout the growing season with a well-balanced houseplant fertilizer.
Humidity	This plant will tolerate a dry atmosphere.
Re-potting	Only re-pot when necessary. Produces a better plant when grown in a shallow container rather than a deep one.
Propagation	Stem cuttings in the spring.

Common names	Golden barrel, Golden ball.
Botanical name	*Echinocactus grusonii.*
Interesting facts	Named after Herman Gruson who owned a large collection of cacti. Name derived from Greek *echinos*, meaning hedgehog.
Origin	Central Mexico.
Position	Full sun especially in the winter months.
Temperature	Minimum winter temperature of 45F.
Watering	Water like a normal houseplant from May to August. In the autumn reduce amount and by October keep almost dry.
Feeding	Feed with balanced houseplant fertilizer from May to August.
Humidity	Do not mist and give plenty of ventilation.
Re-potting	Only re-pot when absolutely necessary.
Propagation	Sow seeds in spring.

Common names	Purple passion vine, Purple velvet plant.
Botanical name	*Gynura sarmentosa.*
Interesting facts	Named from the Greek *gyne*, female and *oura*, a tail, a reference to the long stigma.
Origin	From Malaya to the Philippines.
Position	Good well-lit position in full sun.
Temperature	Minimum winter temperature of 50F.
Watering	Keep moist during the growing season, then reduce the amount in winter.
Feeding	Feed once a month throughout the growing season with a well-balanced houseplant fertilizer.
Humidity	Only the occasional misting is necessary.
Re-potting	Re-pot in the spring if necessary.
Propagation	Stem cuttings from April to August.

Common names	Polka dot plant, Freckle face, Baby's tears.
Botanical name	*Hypoestes phyllostachya.*
Interesting facts	The common name freckle face refers to the pink spots on the leaves.
Origin	Malagasy.
Position	Well-lit in full sun.
Temperature	Minimum winter temperature of 55F.
Watering	The compost should be moist during the growing season, but reduce the amount in winter and keep on the dry side.
Feeding	Throughout the growing season with a nitrogen-rich fertilizer.
Humidity	Mist the leaves frequently and stand pot on a damp gravel tray.
Re-potting	May be necessary every spring.
Propagation	Sow seeds in the spring or propagate from stem cuttings in the summer.

Common name	Beefsteak plant.
Botanical name	*Iresine herbstii.*
Interesting facts	Named after Hermann Carl Gottlieb Herbst, director of the Rio de Janeiro Botanic Gardens.
Origin	South America.
Position	Well-lit but out of direct sunlight.
Temperature	Minimum winter temperature of 55F.
Watering	Keep the compost moist at all times but reduce the amount of watering in winter.
Feeding	Feed with a nitrogen-rich fertilizer from April to September.
Humidity	Stand plant on a damp gravel tray.
Re-potting	Re-pot every spring if necessary.
Propagation	Stem cuttings in the summer months.

Common names	Sensitive plant, Touch-me-not, Humble plant.
Botanical name	*Mimosa pudica.*
Interesting facts	Name derived from the Greek *mimos*, a mimic, a reference to the plant leaves which fold down when touched.
Origin	Tropical America.
Position	Well-lit but out of direct sunlight.
Temperature	Minimum winter temperature of 60F.
Watering	Keep moist during the growing season but reduce watering in winter.
Feeding	Throughout the season with a well-balanced houseplant fertilizer.
Humidity	Stand plant on a damp gravel tray.
Re-potting	Only when necessary in April.
Propagation	Seeds may be difficult to germinate: pour hot water over them before sowing in the early spring.

Common name	Bromeliad.
Botanical name	*Neoregelia carolinae, Nidularium meyendorfii, Aregelia marechalii.*
Interesting facts	Plants may be grown on moss poles or moss trees.
Origin	Brazil.
Position	Well-lit but out of direct sunlight.
Temperature	Minimum winter temperature of 50F.
Watering	Into the rosette of the leaves using rainwater. Only water the compost when this dries out. Empty and refill central rosette every month.
Feeding	Feed from April to September with a well-balanced houseplant fertilizer onto the compost. Ensure the compost is moist before feeding.
Humidity	Mist the leaves frequently in the summer.
Re-potting	Rarely necessary except when plants become top heavy, then re-pot in the spring.
Propagation	Offsets removed in the spring.

Common name	Castor oil plant.
Botanical name	*Ricinus communis.*
Interesting facts	Name derived from the Latin *ricinus*, a tick. The seed is said to resemble a tick.
Origin	Africa.
Position	Well-lit, will tolerate full sun.
Temperature	Minimum winter temperature of 50F.
Watering	Water well during growing season but reduce the amount in winter.
Feeding	Feed with balanced houseplant fertilizer every 2 weeks from April to September.
Humidity	Mist leaves occasionally.
Re-potting	Re-pot every spring if necessary. The plant is frequently grown as an annual.
Propagation	By seed in the spring.

Flowering Plants for Partial or Semi-Shaded Positions

Common names	Urn plant, Vase plant, Silver vase.
Botanical name	*Aechmea fasciata*.
Interesting facts	Name derived from Greek *aichme*, a point, a reference to the rigid parts on the flowers in the bud stage.
Origin	Brazil.
Position	Semi-shade.
Temperature	Minimum winter temperature of 50F.
Watering	Ensure central vase is filled with water, just keep the compost moist.
Feeding	Only occasionally onto the compost, ensuring this is moist before feeding.
Humidity	Mist leaves frequently in the summer.
Re-potting	Only when necessary.
Propagation	By offsets produced in the spring.

Common names	Coral berry, Spiceberry.
Botanical name	*Ardisia crispa.*
Interesting facts	Name derived from the Greek *ardis,* a point. The anthers are spear-shaped.
Origin	South-East Asia.
Position	Semi-shade.
Temperature	Minimum winter temperature of 45F.
Watering	Keep moist at all times during the summer but reduce amount in winter.
Feeding	Feed every 2 weeks from April to September with a nitrogen-rich fertilizer.
Humidity	Mist leaves frequently and stand pot on a damp gravel tray.
Re-potting	When necessary in the spring.
Propagation	Seed sown in the early spring or from cuttings in the summer.

Common name	Trailing Begonia.
Botanical name	*Begonia sutherlandii.*
Interesting facts	The plants were named after the French botanist Michael Begon.
Origin	South Africa.
Position	Semi-shade.
Temperature	Minimum winter temperature of 50F.
Watering	Water well during growing season but allow surface of compost to dry out between waterings.
Feeding	During the growing season with a potash-rich fertilizer.
Humidity	Mist leaves occasionally.
Re-potting	In the spring when necessary.
Propagation	By division.

Common name	Orchid.
Botanical name	*Brassia brachiata (B. verrucosa).*
Interesting facts	Brassia was named for William Bass who collected plants in West Africa for Sir Joseph Banks, who became a close friend of King George III and unofficial director of the Royal Botanic Gardens, Kew.
Origin	Mexico to Venezuela.
Position	Semi-shade.
Temperature	Minimum winter temperature of 55F.
Watering	Water well during the growing season, but allow surface of the compost to dry out between waterings. Reduce amount in winter.
Feeding	Feed with orchid fertilizer according to manufacturer's recommendations.
Humidity	Mist leaves occasionally.
Re-potting	In the spring if necessary into specialized orchid compost.
Propagation	By division.

Common name	Yesterday, today and tomorrow.
Botanical name	*Brunsfelsia latifolia (Franciscea latifolia).*
Interesting facts	Named after Otto Brunfels, a German monk and botanist.
Origin	Tropical Central and South America.
Position	Semi-shade.
Temperature	Minimum winter temperature of 50F.
Watering	Water frequently during the growing season but reduce the amount during the winter months.
Feeding	Throughout the growing season at 14-day intervals with a balanced fertilizer.
Humidity	Mist leaves frequently during the summer.
Re-potting	Re-pot if necessary in the spring.
Propagation	Stem cuttings in the summer months.

Common name	Camellia.
Botanical name	*Camellia* 'Inspiration'.
Interesting facts	Named after George Joseph Kamel, a pharmacist who studied the flora of the Philippines.
Origin	Garden origin.
Position	Semi-shade.
Temperature	Minimum winter temperature of 45F.
Watering	During the growing season keep moist at all times, reduce amount in the winter months.
Feeding	From April to September with a potash-rich fertilizer.
Humidity	Mist leaves occasionally.
Re-potting	Re-pot every spring, if necessary into compost which does not contain lime.
Propagation	Stem cuttings in the spring.

Common name	Cestrum.
Botanical name	*Cestrum elegans (Cestrum purpureum).*
Interesting facts	*Cestrum* is from the Greek word for an unknown species, used by Linnaeus.
Origin	Mexico.
Position	Semi-shade.
Temperature	Minimum winter temperature of 45F.
Watering	During the growing season keep moist. Reduce amount in winter.
Feeding	Feed throughout growing season with a potash-rich fertilizer.
Humidity	Mist leaves occasionally.
Re-potting	Re-pot when necessary in the spring.
Propagation	Stem cuttings in the spring.

Common name	Goldfish plant.
Botanical name	*Columnea gloriosa.*
Interesting facts	Named after Fabius Columna, an Indian botanist and author of the first work to use copperplate illustrations.
Origin	Costa Rica.
Position	Semi-shade.
Temperature	Minimum winter temperature of 50F.
Watering	During the growing season keep the compost moist at all times. Water sparingly during winter.
Feeding	Feed throughout the growing season with a potash-rich fertilizer.
Humidity	Mist leaves frequently, surround pot with damp peat to maintain humidity.
Re-potting	Every 2–3 years in the spring.
Propagation	By stem cutting after flowering.

Common name	Florists' Cyclamen.
Botanical name	*Cyclamen persicum.*
Interesting facts	Derived from the Greek name *Kyklaminos*, from *kyklos*, a circle, referring to the coiled stem of the seed head.
Origin	Southern and eastern regions of the Mediterranean from Algeria to Lebanon, and some Greek islands.
Position	Semi-shade.
Temperature	Minimum winter temperature of 50F.
Watering	Keep compost moist at all times, ensuring that the compost does not dry out.
Feeding	Weekly with a potash-rich fertilizer until the flowers form.
Humidity	Stand pot on a damp gravel tray or surround pot with peat and keep damp.
Re-potting	July into fresh compost. Then start tuber into growth.
Propagation	Seeds sown in July may take up to 12–18 months to flower.

Common name	Angels' trumpet.
Botanical name	*Datura x candida* 'Plena'.
Interesting facts	*Datura* is the Latin version of the Hindustani *dhatura*, or possibly of the Arabic *tatorah*. The plant has very sweetly scented flowers.
Origin	Garden origin. A hybrid between *D. aurea* and *D. versicolor*.
Position	Semi-shade.
Temperature	Minimum winter temperature of 50F.
Watering	Water well during the growing season, keeping compost moist at all times. Reduce the amount in winter.
Feeding	Throughout growing season with a potash-rich fertilizer every 2 weeks from April until September.
Humidity	Mist leaves occasionally.
Re-potting	Re-pot each spring if necessary.
Propagation	By cuttings in late spring and summer.

Common name	Pineapple flower.
Botanical name	*Eucomis comosa (E. punctata).*
Interesting facts	Name derived from the Greek *eu*, good and *kome*, hair. The effect of the leaves resembles a good head of hair.
Origin	South Africa.
Position	Semi-shade.
Temperature	Minimum winter temperature of 45F.
Watering	Water well during the growing season, but allow compost surface to dry out between waterings. Reduce the amount in winter.
Feeding	Every 2 weeks in the growing season with a potash-rich fertilizer.
Humidity	Mist leaves occasionally.
Re-potting	Re-pot every year in the spring.
Propagation	Remove offsets in the spring or sow seeds in the spring.

Common name	Persian violet.
Botanical name	*Exacum affine.*
Interesting facts	Name derived from *exacon,* the Gallic name for *Centaurium,* used by Linnaeus for the genus.
Origin	Socotra (Indian Ocean).
Position	Semi-shade.
Temperature	Minimum winter temperature of 50F.
Watering	Keep the compost moist at all times.
Feeding	Throughout growing season with a potash-rich fertilizer.
Humidity	Stand plants on damp gravel tray and mist leaves frequently.
Re-potting	Normally the plant is thrown away after flowering.
Propagation	Sow seeds in summer.

Common name	Kahili ginger.
Botanical name	*Hedychium gardnerianum.*
Interesting facts	The generic name refers to the first species described. In Greek *hedys* means sweet and *chion* snow and the first species had pure white sweet-smelling flowers.
Origin	Northern India.
Position	Semi-shade.
Temperature	Minimum winter temperature of 50F.
Watering	Water well during the growing season keeping the compost moist at all times. During the winter reduce the amount of water.
Feeding	Every 2 weeks throughout the growing season with a potash-rich fertilizer.
Humidity	Mist leaves frequently.
Re-potting	Every spring if necessary.
Propagation	By division in the spring.

Common name	Common Hydrangea.
Botanical name	*Hydrangea macrophylla (H. hortensis).*
Interesting facts	Name derived from Greek *hydro*, water, and *aggos*, a jar, making reference to the tiny cup-shaped seed capsules.
Origin	Japan.
Position	Semi-shade.
Temperature	Minimum winter temperature of 45F.
Watering	During the growing season keep moist at all times. Reduce the amount over winter. If water contains lime use rainwater.
Feeding	Throughout growing season with a potash-rich fertilizer every 2 weeks.
Humidity	Mist leaves occasionally.
Re-potting	Every spring if necessary, or treat as a short-term pot plant and plant into garden after flowering.
Propagation	Stem cutting in the spring.

Common name	Busy Lizzie.
Botanical name	*Impatiens* 'New Guinea Hybrids'.
Interesting facts	Name derived from the Latin *impatiens*, meaning impatient, referring to the way the seed explodes and scatters from some species.
Origin	Garden origin.
Position	Semi-shade.
Temperature	Minimum winter temperature of 55F.
Watering	Throughout the growing season keep moist at all times. Reduce the amount in winter.
Feeding	Every week throughout the growing season with a potash-rich fertilizer.
Humidity	Mist the leaves occasionally, but not when the plant is in flower.
Re-potting	Only when pot-bound in the spring. Over-potting results in foliage growth at the expense of flowers.
Propagation	Seeds or cuttings in the spring.

Common name	Lantana.
Botanical name	*Lanata sellowiana* *(L. montevidensis).*
Interesting facts	*Lantana* is an ancient name for viburnum, as the foliage of the 2 shrubs looks similar.
Origin	South America.
Position	Semi-shade.
Temperature	Minimum winter temperature of 55F.
Watering	Keep the compost moist throughout the growing season, allowing the surface to dry out between waterings. Reduce the amount in the winter, sparingly in the spring.
Feeding	Every 2 weeks throughout the growing season with a potash-rich fertilizer.
Humidity	Mist leaves occasionally.
Re-potting	Re-pot if necessary in the spring.
Propagation	Sow seeds in the spring or stem cuttings in the summer.

Common name	Chilean bell flower.
Botanical name	*Lapageria rosea.*
Interesting facts	Named after Josephine de la Pagerie, Napoleon's Empress.
Origin	Central Chile.
Position	Semi-shade.
Temperature	Minimum winter temperature of 40F.
Watering	Allow compost surface to dry out between waterings.
Feeding	Every 2 weeks throughout the growing season with a potash-rich fertilizer.
Humidity	Mist leaves occasionally.
Re-potting	Only when necessary.
Propagation	Sow seeds in the spring after soaking in water for 48 hours.

Common name	Pink allamanda.
Botanical name	*Mandevilla splendens (Dipladenia sanderi).*
Interesting facts	*Mandevilla* was named after Henry John Mandeville, a British minister in Argentina who introduced the first species into cultivation.
Origin	Brazil.
Position	Semi-shade.
Temperature	Minimum winter temperature of 55F.
Watering	Water regularly throughout the growing season, sparingly during winter.
Feeding	Every 2 weeks throughout the growing season with a balanced houseplant fertilizer.
Humidity	Mist plant regularly especially when buds are forming and stand plant on a damp gravel tray.
Re-potting	Re-pot every year in the spring.
Propagation	Stem cutting in the spring.

Common name	Peristrophe.
Botanical name	*Peristrophe speciosa*.
Interesting facts	Name derived from the Greek *peri*, around and *strophe*, twist, referring to the twisted corolla lobes.
Origin	India.
Position	Semi-shade.
Temperature	Minimum winter temperature of 50F.
Watering	Water well throughout growing season but allow the compost surface to dry out between waterings. Reduce the amount during the winter.
Feeding	Every 2 weeks throughout growing season with balanced houseplant fertilizer.
Humidity	Mist leaves occasionally.
Re-potting	When necessary in the spring.
Propagation	Stem cuttings in the spring.

Common name	Fairy primrose.
Botanical name	*Primula malacoides.*
Interesting facts	*Malacoides* means mallow-like.
Origin	Western China.
Position	Semi-shade.
Temperature	Minimum winter temperature of 55F.
Watering	Keep plants moist especially during the flowering period.
Feeding	Feed every 2 weeks throughout the growing season with a balanced houseplant fertilizer.
Humidity	Mist leaves occasionally and place plant on a damp gravel tray.
Re-potting	Normally grown as an annual and potted into a 3.5 inch pot then into a 5 inch pot and thrown away after flowering is completed.
Propagation	Seeds sown in June or July.

Common name	African violet.
Botanical name	*Saintpaulia ionantha.*
Interesting facts	Named after Baron Walter von Saint Paul Illaire, who found the first species.
Origin	Coastal Tanzania.
Position	Semi-shade, but well-lit spot during the winter months. For winter blooms 14 hours of artificial light is necessary.
Temperature	Minimum winter temperature of 55F.
Watering	Keep compost moist, but allow surface of compost to dry between waterings. Reduce amount of watering during the winter months.
Feeding	Every 2 weeks with a specialist *Saintpaulia* fertilizer.
Humidity	Do not wet foliage, place plant on a damp gravel tray.
Re-potting	Re-pot if necessary in the spring.
Propagation	Leaf cuttings in the spring or sow seeds.

Common name	Christmas cactus.
Botanical name	*Schlumbergia x buckleyi.*
Interesting facts	Named after Frederick Schlumberger, a Belgian grower, explorer and plant collector.
Origin	Garden hybrid.
Position	Semi-shade.
Temperature	Minimum winter temperature of 55F.
Watering	Water well throughout the growing season, allowing the surface to dry out between waterings. Just keep moist in the winter.
Feeding	Every 2 weeks throughout the growing season with a balanced houseplant fertilizer.
Humidity	Mist leaves frequently.
Re-potting	Annually once flowering has finished.
Propagation	Cuttings taken between April and August. Allow cuttings to dry before putting them into the compost.

Common names	Peace lily, White sails.
Botanical name	*Spathiphyllum wallisii.*
Interesting facts	Name derived from the Greek *spathe*, bract (looking like a flower) and *phyllon*, leaf, the spathes being leaf-like in shape.
Origin	Colombia and Venezuela.
Position	Semi-shade.
Temperature	Minimum winter temperature of 55F.
Watering	Keep compost moist during growing season, and reduce the amount in winter.
Feeding	Throughout growing season with a potash-rich fertilizer.
Humidity	Stand plant on a damp gravel tray.
Re-potting	Every year in the spring.
Propagation	Divide plant at re-potting time.

Common name	Bird of paradise flower.
Botanical name	*Strelitzia reginae.*
Interesting facts	Named after Charlotte of Mecklenburg-Strelitz, who became the queen of George III.
Origin	South Africa.
Position	Semi-shade.
Temperature	Minimum winter temperature of 55F.
Watering	Water well throughout the growing season. Allow surface of compost to dry out between waterings, sparingly in the winter.
Feeding	Once every month with a potash-rich fertilizer.
Humidity	Do not wet foliage. Stand plant on a damp gravel tray.
Re-potting	Re-pot every year in the spring if necessary.
Propagation	Division of plant in spring when re-potting.

Common name	Marmalade bush.
Botanical name	*Streptosolen jamesonii.*
Interesting facts	Named derived from Greek *streptos*, twisted and *solen*, a tube, referring to the twisted corolla tubes.
Origin	Colombia, Ecuador.
Position	Semi-shade.
Temparature	Minimum winter temperature of 50F.
Watering	Water well throughout growing season. Allow the surface of the compost to dry between waterings and reduce the amount in winter.
Feeding	Every 2 weeks throughout the growing season with a potash-rich fertilizer.
Humidity	Mist leaves occasionally.
Re-potting	In the spring if necessary.
Propagation	Cuttings of young shoots in the late spring.

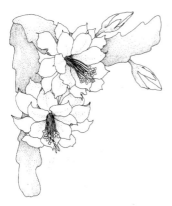

Foliage Plants for Semi-Shaded Positions

Common name	Chinese evergreen.
Botanical name	*Aglanonema* 'Silver Queen'.
Interesting facts	Name derived from the Greek *aglaos*, bright and *nema*, a thread, referring to the stamens. Grows best in a shallow pot.
Origin	Garden origin.
Position	Semi-shade.
Temperature	Minimum winter temperature of 60F.
Watering	During growing season water well, at other times of the year water sparingly.
Feeding	Every 2 weeks throughout the growing season with a nitrogen-rich houseplant fertilizer.
Humidity	Stand plant on a damp gravel tray and mist frequently.
Re-potting	Normally on a 3-year basis in the spring.
Propagation	Division in the spring.

Common name	Plume asparagus.
Botanical name	*Asparagus densiflorus (A. meyeri).*
Interesting facts	Name said to be derived from the Greek *intensive*, and *sparasso*, to tear, alluding to the prickles of some species.
Origin	South Africa.
Position	Semi-shade.
Temperature	Minimum winter temperature of 50F.
Watering	Best watered from base, regularly from spring to autumn but sparingly during winter.
Feeding	Every 2 weeks throughout the growing season with a nitrogen-rich houseplant fertilizer.
Humidity	Mist leaves occasionally.
Re-potting	Re-pot annually in the spring.
Propagation	Division in the spring or seeds in the spring.

Common name	Begonia.
Botanical name	*Begonia* Caribbean Hybrid.
Interesting facts	The genus was named after Michael Begon, patron of botany and once governor of French Canada.
Origin	Garden hybrid.
Position	Semi-shade.
Temperature	Minimum winter temperature of 55F.
Watering	Keep compost moist during the growing season but allow the compost to dry out between waterings. Water sparingly in the winter.
Feeding	Every 2 weeks throughout the growing season with a nitrogen-rich houseplant fertilizer.
Humidity	Stand plant on a damp gravel tray. Do not mist the leaves.
Re-potting	Annually in the spring.
Propagation	Division in the spring.

Common names	Spider plant, St Bernard's lily.
Botanical name	*Chlorophytum comosus variegatum (Anthericum comosus).*
Interesting facts	Name derived from Greek, *clideios,* delicate and *anthos,* a flower or *phytum,* a plant.
Origin	South Africa.
Position	Semi-shade.
Temperature	Minimum winter temperature of 45F.
Watering	Water well during the growing season, reduce the amount in winter.
Feeding	Every 2 weeks throughout the growing season with a nitrogen-rich houseplant fertilizer.
Humidity	Mist leaves occasionally.
Re-potting	Each spring.
Propagation	Peg down plantlets into compost when these are produced, cut through stem when rooted, or divide plants in the spring.

Common name	Ti tree.
Botanical name	*Cordyline terminalis* 'Kiwi'.
Interesting facts	*Cordyline* derives from *cordyle,* a club, referring to the swollen stem bases of some species which result in a somewhat club-like appearance.
Origin	Tropical Asia, Polynesia.
Position	Semi-shade.
Temperature	Minimum winter temperature of 55F.
Watering	Keep compost moist at all times, reduce the amount in the winter, but do not dry off completely.
Feeding	Every 2 weeks throughout the growing season with a nitrogen-rich houseplant fertilizer.
Humidity	Mist leaves frequently.
Re-potting	When necessary.
Propagation	Suckers detached in the late spring, or 2 inch long sections of stem in early summer, treat as cuttings.

Common names	Finger aralia, False aralia.
Botanical name	*Dizygotheca elegantissima (Aralia elegantissima).*
Interesting facts	Named from Greek *dis*, twice, *zygos*, a yoke and *theka*, a case. The anthers have four lobes, twice the normal number.
Origin	New Caledonia, Polynesia, Australasia.
Position	Semi-shade.
Temperature	Minimum winter temperature of 60F.
Watering	Only moderately during the growing season. Keep on the dry side during winter.
Feeding	Every 2 weeks throughout the growing season with a nitrogen-rich houseplant fertilizer.
Humidity	Stand plant on a damp gravel tray and mist leaves frequently.
Re-potting	Every 2 years in the spring.
Propagation	From imported seeds in the spring, or by air-layering. In the summer by stem section cuttings.

Common name	False palm.
Botanical name	*Dracaena deremensis* 'Yellow'.
Interesting facts	Name derived from the Greek *drakainia*, a dragon. Also suggested that it was named after Sir Francis Drake.
Origin	Tropical Africa.
Position	Semi-shade.
Temperature	Minimum winter temperature of 55F.
Watering	Keep the compost moist at all times. Reduce the amount during winter, but do not allow to dry out completely.
Feeding	Every 2 weeks throughout the growing season with a nitrogen-rich houseplant fertilizer.
Humidity	Mist leaves frequently.
Re-potting	Every 2 years.
Propagation	Stem section cuttings in the spring or stem tip cuttings in late spring .

Common name	Ribbon plant.
Botanical name	*Dracaena sanderiana.*
Interesting facts	See *Dracaena deremensis* p94.
Origin	Central Africa.
Position	Semi-shade.
Temperature	Minimum winter temperature of 55F.
Watering	See *D. deremensis.*
Feeding	Every 2 weeks throughout the growing season with a nitrogen-rich houseplant fertilizer.
Humidity	Mist the leaves frequently and stand plant on a damp gravel tray.
Re-potting	Every 2 years.
Propagation	Stem cuttings in the spring or stem tip cuttings in the late spring.

Common name	False castor-oil plant.
Botanical name	*Fatsia japonica (Aralia japonica, A. sieboldii)*.
Interesting facts	*Fatsia* is the Latinized version of *fatsi*, said to be the Japanese name for the plant.
Origin	Japan, South Korea.
Position	Semi-shade.
Temperature	Minimum winter temperature of 40F.
Watering	Water frequently in the growing season but reduce the amount in winter.
Feeding	Every 2 weeks throughout the growing season with a nitrogen-rich houseplant fertilizer.
Humidity	Stand the plant on a damp gravel tray.
Re-potting	Every spring.
Propagation	From seeds in the late spring or stem cuttings in the summer.

Common name	Golden false castor-oil plant.
Botanical name	*Fatsia japonica* Gold.
Interesting facts	See *Fatsia japonica*.
Origin	Japan, South Korea.
Position	Semi-shade.
Temperature	Minimum winter temperature of 40F.
Watering	See *F. japonica*.
Feeding	Every 2 weeks throughout the growing season with a nitrogen-rich houseplant fertilizer.
Humidity	Stand plant on a damp gravel tray.
Re-potting	Every spring.
Propagation	Stem cuttings in the summer.

Common name	Weeping fig.
Botanical name	*Ficus benjamina.*
Interesting facts	Do not move the plant often or the leaves tend to drop off.
Origin	Tropical Asia.
Position	Semi-shade.
Temperature	Minimum winter temperature of 55F.
Watering	Water well but allow the surface of the compost to dry between waterings during the growing season. Reduce the amount in the winter.
Feeding	Every 2 weeks throughout the growing season with a nitrogen-rich houseplant fertilizer.
Humidity	Stand the plant on a damp gravel tray during the summer.
Re-potting	Only when necessary.
Propagation	Stem tip cuttings during the summer.

Common name	Rubber plant.
Botanical name	*Ficus elastica.*
Interesting facts	*Elastica* means producing elastic.
Origin	India, Malaysia.
Position	Semi-shade.
Temperature	Minimum winter temperature of 55F.
Watering	Water well during the growing season, but allow the surface of the compost to dry out between waterings. Reduce the amount in winter.
Feeding	Every 2 weeks throughout the growing season with a nitrogen-rich houseplant fertilizer.
Humidity	Stand the plant on a damp gravel tray.
Re-potting	Only when necessary.
Propagation	Air-layering in the summer, leaf bud cuttings or stem tip cuttings.

Common names	Rubber plant, Fig tree.
Botanical name	*Ficus elastica* 'Belga'.
Interesting facts	Fruits not normally produced on pot plants. The plants require plenty of space. *Fikus* is the Latin name for a fig tree. Believed to be from the Hebrew name, *Fag*.
Origin	India, Malaysia.
Position	Partially shaded.
Temperature	Minimum winter temperature 55F.
Watering	Allow compost to dry out between waterings. During the winter months just keep damp – not wet.
Feeding	From April to September with a balanced houseplant fertilizer.
Humidity	Mist leaves occasionally.
Re-potting	Plants grow better when slightly pot-bound. Re-pot every 2–3 years in the spring if necessary.
Propagation	Air-layer, leaf bud cuttings, stem cuttings.

Common names	Creeping fig, Climbing fig.
Botanical name	*Ficus pumila.*
Interesting facts	Normally grown as a creeping plant but also climbs.
Origin	Eastern Asia, Australia.
Position	Semi-shade.
Temperature	Minimum winter temperature of 55F.
Watering	Water well during the growing season, but reduce the amount in winter.
Feeding	Every 2 weeks throughout the growing season with a nitrogen-rich houseplant fertilizer.
Humidity	Stand the plant on a damp gravel tray and mist the leaves frequently.
Re-potting	Only when necessary.
Propagation	Stem tip cuttings in the summer.

Common name	Herringbone plant.
Botanical name	*Maranta* 'Tricolor', *M. leuconeura erythrophylla*.
Interesting facts	*Maranta* was named after Bartolommeo Maranti, an Italian physician and botanist.
Origin	Tropical America.
Position	Semi-shade.
Temperature	Minimum winter temperature of 50F.
Watering	Keep the compost moist during the growing season but allow the compost to dry out in winter.
Feeding	Every 2 weeks throughout the growing season with a nitrogen-rich houseplant fertilizer.
Humidity	Stand the plant on a damp gravel tray and mist the leaves frequently.
Re-potting	Only when necessary.
Propagation	Division in the spring.

Common names	Swiss cheese plant, Split leaf philodendron, Mexican bread fruit, Ceriman.
Botanical name	*Monstera deliciosa*.
Interesting facts	Derivation of first name is obscure, probably from *monstifer*, monster-bearing, referring to holes in plant leaves, which are large. Second name refers to the delicious fruits.
Origin	Mexico, Central America.
Position	Light shade.
Temperature	Active growth occurs at 65F, over winter at a minimum of 50F.
Watering	During November to March keep the soil moist; rest of the year water regularly ensuring pot is damp.
Feeding	Weekly from late March through to September with a balanced houseplant fertilizer.
Humidity	Mist leaves frequently throughout growing season. Wash dust off leaves occasionally.
Re-potting	Necessary every 2–3 years in April.
Propagation	Stem tip cuttings or air-layer.

Common name	Bead plant.
Botanical name	*Nertera granadensis*.
Interesting facts	*Nertera* derives from the Greek *nerteros*, lowly, referring to its low habit of growth.
Origin	Mexico and Central America.
Position	Semi-shade.
Temperature	Minimum winter temperature of 40F.
Watering	Keep compost moist during the growing season but reduce the amount in winter.
Feeding	Every 2 weeks throughout the growing season with a nitrogen-rich houseplant fertilizer.
Humidity	Mist the leaves occasionally.
Re-potting	Only when necessary, however the plant is normally thrown away after the beads have dropped off.
Propagation	Division in the spring.

Common name	Song of India.
Botanical name	*Pleomele reflexa variegata (Draceana reflexa).*
Interesting facts	*Reflexa* refers to the curled back flowers.
Origin	Madagascar, Mauritius.
Position	Semi-shade.
Temperature	Minimum winter temperature of 55F.
Watering	Keep the compost moist at all times. Reduce the amount in winter, but do not allow to dry out completely.
Feeding	Every 2 weeks throughout the growing season with a nitrogen-rich houseplant fertilizer.
Humidity	Mist leaves frequently.
Re-potting	Every 2 years.
Propagation	Stem section cuttings in the spring.

Common name	Radermachera.
Botanical name	*Radermachera sinica* 'Danielle' *(Stereospermum sinicum)*.
Interesting facts	*Radermachera* commemorates J.C.M. Radermacher, a Dutch amateur botanist.
Origin	China.
Position	Semi-shade.
Temperature	Minimum winter temperature of 55F.
Watering	Keep compost moist at all times, but do not over-water in the winter.
Feeding	Every 2 weeks throughout the growing season with a nitrogen-rich houseplant fertilizer.
Humidity	This plant will tolerate a dry atmosphere, so misting is not necessary.
Re-potting	Only when necessary.
Propagation	By imported seed from China in summer.

Common name	Grape Ivy.
Botanical name	*Rhoicissus rhomboidea.*
Interesting facts	What is normally sold under this name is *Cissus rhombifolia*, as this species is not usually in cultivation.
Origin	South Africa.
Position	Semi-shade.
Temperature	Minimum winter temperature of 45F.
Watering	Water well during the growing season but reduce the amount in winter.
Feeding	Every 2 weeks throughout the growing season with a nitrogen-rich houseplant fertilizer.
Humidity	Mist the leaves occasionally.
Re-potting	When necessary in the spring.
Propagation	Stem cuttings in the spring or summer.

Common names	Mother-in-law's tongue, Snake plant.
Botanical name	*Sansevieria trifaciata laurentii.*
Interesting facts	The plant was named after Prince Raimond de Sanagrio de Sanseviero.
Origin	South Africa.
Position	Semi-shade.
Temperature	Minimum winter temperature of 50F.
Watering	Water moderately during the growing season, allowing the compost to dry between waterings, in winter only every 1–2 months.
Feeding	Every 2 weeks throughout the growing season with a nitrogen-rich houseplant fertilizer.
Humidity	This plant will tolerate a fairly dry atmosphere. Do not allow water to enter the heart of the plant.
Re-potting	This plant grows better if pot-bound, only re-pot when the roots crack the pot.
Propagation	By division in the spring.

Common names	Variegated mother of thousands, Strawberry geranium.
Botanical name	*Saxifraga sarmentosa* 'Tricolor' *(Saxifraga stolonifera)*.
Interesting facts	The name reflects the habit of the plant in producing lots of overground stems.
Origin	Eastern Asia.
Position	Semi-shade.
Temperature	Minimum winter temperature of 40F.
Watering	Water well during the growing season. During the winter allow the surface of the compost to dry out between waterings.
Feeding	Every 2 weeks throughout the growing season with a nitrogen-rich houseplant fertilizer.
Humidity	Mist the leaves occasionally.
Re-potting	Every year in the spring.
Propagation	Peg down the plantlets during the growing season.

Common name	Stromanthe.
Botanical name	*Stomanthe amadilis, (Calathea amadilis, Maranta amabilis).*
Interesting facts	Named from the Greek *stroma*, a bed and *anthos*, a flower, reflecting the shape of the flower.
Origin	Brazil.
Position	Semi-shade.
Temperature	Minimum winter temperature of 50F.
Watering	Keep the compost moist throughout the growing season, but reduce the amount in winter.
Feeding	Every 2 weeks throughout the growing season with a nitrogen-rich houseplant fertilizer.
Humidity	Stand the pot on a damp gravel tray and mist the leaves frequently.
Re-potting	Every 2 years.
Propagation	Divide the plant in the spring.

Common name	Syngonium.
Botanical name	*Syngonium hoffmannii* hybrid *(Nephthytis hoffmannii)*.
Interesting facts	*Syngonium* is derived from the Greek *syn*, together and *gone,* womb, an allusion to the united ovaries.
Origin	Garden origin.
Position	Semi-shade.
Temperature	Minimum winter temperature of 55F.
Watering	Keep the compost moist at all times during the growing season, but allow the surface of the compost to dry out between waterings in the winter.
Feeding	Every 2 weeks throughout the growing season with a nitrogen-rich houseplant fertilizer.
Humidity	Stand the pot on a damp gravel tray and mist the leaves frequently.
Re-potting	Every 2 years.
Propagation	Stem cuttings in the summer.

Common names	Goosefoot plant, Arrowhead vine.
Botanical name	*Syngonium podophyllum.*
Interesting facts	See *Syngonium hoffmannii* p111.
Origin	Mexico to Panama.
Position	Semi-shade.
Temperature	Minimum winter temperature of 55F.
Watering	See *S. hoffmannii.*
Feeding	Every 2 weeks throughout the growing season with a nitrogen-rich houseplant fertilizer.
Humidity	See *S. hoffmannii.*
Re-potting	Every 2 years.
Propagation	Stem cuttings in the summer.

Common names	Pick-a-back or Piggyback plant.
Botanical name	*Tolmiea menziesii.*
Interesting facts	Named after Dr William Fraser Tolmie, a surgeon to the Hudson Bay Company based in Fort Vancouver.
Origin	Western North America.
Position	Semi-shade.
Temperature	Minimum winter temperature of 40F.
Watering	Keep the compost moist during the growing season but reduce the amount in winter.
Feeding	Every 2 weeks throughout the growing season with a nitrogen-rich houseplant fertilizer.
Humidity	Mist the leaves occasionally.
Re-potting	Every year in the spring.
Propagation	Peg down the young plantlets during the summer.

Plants for Shaded Positions

Common name	Delta maidenhead fern.
Botanical name	*Adiantum raddianum (A. cuneatum, A. aemulum).*
Interesting facts	Name derived from the Greek *adiantos*, dry or unwetted, referring to the water-repellent nature of the fronds.
Origin	Tropical America.
Position	Shade.
Temperature	Minimum winter temperature of 50F.
Watering	Never allow the compost to dry out – it should be moist but not soggy.
Feeding	Every 2 weeks throughout the growing season with a nitrogen-rich houseplant fertilizer.
Humidity	Stand the plant on a damp gravel tray and mist the leaves frequently.
Re-potting	Re-pot in spring only when necessary. Do not plant too deeply.
Propagation	Division of the plant in the spring or by spores.

Common names	Painter's palette, Tailflower.
Botanical name	*Anthurium andreanum.*
Interesting facts	Name derived from *anthos*, a flower and *oura*, tail, from the shape of the spadix.
Origin	Colombia.
Position	Shade.
Temperature	Minimum winter temperature of 60F.
Watering	Keep compost moist at all times, but do not allow compost to become soggy, especially during winter.
Feeding	Every 2 weeks throughout the growing season with a nitrogen-rich houseplant fertilizer.
Humidity	Stand the plant on a damp gravel tray and mist the leaves frequently.
Re-potting	When necessary in spring.
Propagation	Division in the spring.

Common name	Bird's nest fern.
Botanical name	*Asplenium nidus (A. nidus-avis)*.
Interesting facts	Historically thought to have been used medicinally for curing problems with the spleen.
Origin	Tropical Asia, Australia.
Position	Shade.
Temperature	Minimum winter temperature of 50F.
Watering	Keep compost moist at all times, but do not allow to become soggy in winter.
Feeding	Every 2 weeks throughout the growing season with a nitrogen-rich houseplant fertilizer.
Humidity	Stand the plant on a damp gravel tray and mist the leaves frequently.
Re-potting	Only when necessary in the spring.
Propagation	Division in the spring or by spores.

Common names	Painted leaf, fan begonia.
Botanical name	*Begonia rex.*
Interesting facts	Most of the named forms with good leaf colour are garden hybrids.
Origin	Assam.
Position	Shade.
Temperature	Minimum winter temperature of 50F.
Watering	Keep moist during the growing season, but allow the surface of the compost to dry out between waterings in winter.
Feeding	Every 2 weeks throughout the growing season with a nitrogen-rich houseplant fertilizer.
Humidity	Stand the plant on a damp gravel tray and mist the leaves frequently.
Re-potting	Annually in the spring. Pot-bound plants lose their colour.
Propagation	Division of plants in the spring.

Common name	Angel's wings.
Botanical name	*Caladium hortulanum* 'Frieda Hemple'.
Interesting facts	Name derived from the vernacular name *Kaladi*, misused for this genus.
Origin	Garden origin.
Position	Shade.
Temperature	Minimum winter temperature of 60F.
Watering	Water well keeping compost moist during the growing season.
Feeding	Every 2 weeks throughout the growing season with a nitrogen-rich houseplant fertilizer.
Humidity	Stand the plant on a damp gravel tray and mist the leaves frequently.
Re-potting	Leaves die down in September. Stop watering and allow tubers to dry. Re-plant tubers in March and water well.
Propagation	By offsets or division of tubers in the spring.

Common name	Dumb cane.
Botanical name	*Dieffenbachia picta* 'Camilla' *(D. maculata).*
Interesting facts	The plant is poisonous and the sap should be kept away from skin, mouth and eyes.
Origin	Garden origin.
Position	Shade.
Temperature	Minimum winter temperature of 60F.
Watering	Water frequently during the growing season but allow the compost surface to dry out between waterings in winter.
Feeding	Every 2 weeks throughout the growing season with a nitrogen-rich houseplant fertilizer.
Humidity	Stand the plant on a damp gravel tray and mist the leaves frequently.
Re-potting	Every spring.
Propagation	Stem section cuttings.

Common name	Dumb cane.
Botanical name	*Dieffenbachia picta.*
Interesting facts	The plant is poisonous. Named after J. P. Diffenbach, the administrator of the Royal Palace Gardens in Vienna.
Origin	Brazil.
Position	Shade.
Temperature	Minimum winter temperature of 60F.
Watering	See *D. picta* 'Camilla'.
Feeding	Every 2 weeks throughout the growing season with a nitrogen-rich houseplant fertilizer.
Humidity	Stand the plant on a damp gravel tray and mist the leaves frequently.
Re-potting	Every spring.
Propagation	Stem section cuttings.

Common names	Painted net leaf, Nerve plant.
Botanical name	*Fittonia verschaffeltii* Red and Silver.
Interesting facts	*Fittonia* was named after Elizabeth and Sarah Mary Fitton who wrote *Conversations on Botany* in 1817.
Origin	Peru.
Position	Shade.
Temperature	Minimum winter temperature of 60F.
Watering	Water well during the growing season, but allow the surface of the compost to dry out between waterings in winter.
Feeding	Every 2 weeks throughout the growing season with a nitrogen-rich houseplant fertilizer.
Humidity	Stand the plant on a damp gravel tray and mist the leaves frequently.
Re-potting	Re-pot every spring.
Propagation	Division in the spring.

Common name	Ivy.
Botanical name	*Hedera helix*.
Interesting facts	*Helix* is thought to refer to the legend that the plant was wound around a staff carried by the wine-god Bacchus and his attendants.
Origin	Europe to the Caucasus.
Position	Shade.
Temperature	Minimum winter temperature of 45F.
Watering	Keep moist in the summer but allow surface of the compost to dry out between waterings in winter.
Feeding	Every 2 weeks throughout the growing season with a nitrogen-rich houseplant fertilizer.
Humidity	Stand the plant on a damp gravel tray and mist the leaves frequently.
Re-potting	When necessary in the spring.
Propagation	Cuttings in the spring.

Common name	Boston fern.
Botanical name	*Nephrolepis exaltata* *'Bostoniensis'*.
Interesting facts	Name derived from the Greek *nephros*, a kidney and *lepis*, a scale which covers the spores.
Origin	Garden origin.
Position	Shade.
Temperature	Minimum winter temperature of 50F.
Watering	Keep the compost moist at all times, but do not allow it to become soggy in winter.
Feeding	Every 2 weeks throughout the growing season with a nitrogen-rich houseplant fertilizer.
Humidity	Stand the plant on a damp gravel tray and mist the leaves frequently.
Re-potting	Only when necessary in the spring.
Propagation	By division or spores in the spring.

Common names	Sweetheart plant, Heart leaf.
Botanical name	*Philodendron scandens.*
Interesting facts	Name derived from the Greek *philos*, love and *dendron*, a tree.
Origin	Tropical America.
Position	Shade.
Temperature	Minimum winter temperature of 50F.
Watering	Water well during the growing season but keep compost just moist in the winter.
Feeding	Every 2 weeks throughout the growing season with a nitrogen-rich houseplant fertilizer.
Humidity	Stand the plant on a damp gravel tray and mist the leaves frequently.
Re-potting	Every 3 years.
Propagation	Cuttings in the spring.

Common name	Aluminium plant.
Botanical name	*Pilea cadierei.*
Interesting facts	*Pilea* derives from the Latin name *pileus*, a cap.
Origin	Vietnam.
Position	Shade.
Temperature	Minimum winter temperature of 50F.
Watering	Water well during the growing season but allow surface of the compost to dry out between waterings in winter.
Feeding	Every 2 weeks throughout the growing season with a nitrogen-rich houseplant fertilizer.
Humidity	Stand the plant on a damp gravel tray and mist the leaves frequently.
Re-potting	In the spring if necessary.
Propagation	Division in the spring or summer.

Common name	Staghorn fern.
Botanical name	*Platycerium bifurcatum (P. alcicorne).*
Interesting facts	Name derived from the Greek, *platys,* broad and *keros,* a horn, alluding to the shape of the fronds.
Origin	Eastern Australia to Polynesia.
Position	Shade.
Temperature	Minimum winter temperature of 50F.
Watering	Never allow the compost to dry out, but it should not be soggy in the winter.
Feeding	Every 2 weeks throughout the growing season with a nitrogen-rich houseplant fertilizer.
Humidity	Stand the plant on a damp gravel tray and mist the leaves frequently.
Re-potting	Only when necessary.
Propagation	Division in the summer .

Common name	Sword brake.
Botanical name	*Pteris ensiformis 'Victoriae'*.
Interesting facts	From the Greek *pteron*, a wing.
Origin	Eastern Asia to Australia.
Position	Shade.
Temperature	Minimum winter temperature of 50F.
Watering	Never allow compost to dry out, but it should not become soggy in winter.
Feeding	Every 2 weeks throughout the growing season with a nitrogen-rich houseplant fertilizer.
Humidity	Stand the plant on a damp gravel tray and mist the leaves frequently.
Re-potting	In the spring when necessary.
Propagation	Division or from spores.

Common names	Devil's ivy, Golden pathos, Tar vine.
Botanical name	*Scindapsus aureus, Rhaphidophora aurea, Epipremnum aureum.*
Interesting facts	*Scindapsus* is the ancient Greek name for a plant looking like an ivy.
Origin	Solomon Islands.
Position	Shade.
Temperature	Minimum winter temperature of 50F.
Watering	Water well during the growing season but allow the compost to dry out between waterings in the winter.
Feeding	Every 2 weeks throughout the growing season with a nitrogen-rich houseplant fertilizer.
Humidity	Stand the plant on a damp gravel tray and mist the leaves frequently.
Re-potting	When necessary in the spring.
Propagation	Stem cuttings in the spring or summer.

Common name	Devil's ivy.
Botanical name	*Scindapsus aureus* 'Marble Queen'.
Interesting facts	See *S. aureus.*, p130
Origin	Garden origin.
Position	Shade.
Temperature	Minimum winter temperature of 50F.
Watering	See *S. aureus.*
Feeding	Every 2 weeks throughout the growing season with a nitrogen-rich houseplant fertilizer.
Humidity	Stand the plant on a damp gravel tray and mist the leaves frequently.
Re-potting	When necessary in the spring.
Propagation	Stem cuttings in the spring or summer.

Common name	Creeping moss.
Botanical name	*Selaginella.*
Interesting facts	Name derived from Latin *selago*, the name for the common or club moss of the northern temperate zone.
Origin	Mainly tropical.
Position	Shade.
Temperature	Minimum winter temperature of 55F.
Watering	Keep compost moist throughout the growing season, reduce the amount of water in winter and allow compost surface to dry out between winter waterings.
Feeding	Every 2 weeks throughout the growing season with a nitrogen-rich houseplant fertilizer.
Humidity	Stand the plant on a damp gravel tray and mist the leaves frequently.
Re-potting	When necessary in the spring.
Propagation	Stem cuttings in the spring.

GLOSSARY

Terms

Anther Pollen bearing part of a stamen

Annual A plant which germinates, flowers and sets seed in one growing season

Corolla tube A collective term for the petals forming a tube

Hybrid A plant originating by the fertilization of one species by another. The sign X between a plant name depicts that the plant is a hybrid

Offsets Short lateral shoots bearing close rosettes of leaves, which are capable of taking root and being separated from the mother plant

Plantlet Young plant, quite often produced at the end of a long stem, can be rooted

Pot-bound Is the situation when the roots of a plant are coming out from the drainage holes and have started to curl around the inside of the pot

Rhizome A more or less swollen stem, wholly or partially underground

Stamens Male pollen-bearing part of the flower

Spores Minute reproductive body of a non-flowering plant

Stolons Creeping stems which often form new plants on it above ground level

Suckers A shoot arising adventurously from a root of a plant often at some distance from the main stem

Tuber Swollen, underground part of stem or root

Techniques

Air-layering A slanting cut is made into the stem of the plant near the growing point. This is then surrounded with moss and covered with plastic. Rooting then takes place into the moss and the rooted portion is then detached

Division The operation which involves separating a plant up into smaller sections. With houseplants this is normally done with the hands

Layering Long stems are bent down into the soil to form a 'U' shape. The base of the 'U' is cut partly through. From this region roots appear

Leaf-bud cuttings Cuttings which consist of a leaf, its axillary bud and a portion of stem

Leaf-section cuttings Cuttings which consist of a leaf or portion of the leaf excluding the axillary bud or portion of stem

Re-pot (repotting) To transfer a plant from one plant pot into another either of the same size or one slightly larger which contains fresh compost

Softwood cuttings (stem tip cuttings) Cuttings which are prepared from a young shoot which is still extending

Stem cutting (stem section cutting) The cutting up of portions of the stem which then become cuttings inserted into compost

Pegging down plantlets This involves the use of a piece of wire bent to form a 'U' shaped pin which is then turned upside down and positioned over the stem with the plantlet on the end, into cutting compost until the plantlet is rooted. Once rooted the pin and parent plant's stem are removed leaving a newly rooted plant

INDEX OF COMMON NAMES

INDEX OF BOTANICAL NAMES